BRAZIL AND THE UNITED STATES

AEI-Hoover
policy studies

The studies in this series are issued jointly
by the American Enterprise Institute
for Public Policy Research and the Hoover
Institution on War, Revolution and Peace.
They are designed to focus on
policy problems of current and future interest,
to set forth the factors underlying
these problems and to evaluate
courses of action available to policymakers.
The views expressed in these studies
are those of the authors and do not necessarily
reflect the views of the staff, officers
or members of the governing boards of
AEI or the Hoover Institution.

BRAZIL
AND THE UNITED STATES

Toward a maturing relationship

Roger W. Fontaine

American Enterprise Institute for Public Policy Research
Washington, D. C.

Hoover Institution on War, Revolution and Peace
Stanford University, Stanford, California

AEI-Hoover Policy Study 13, December 1974
(Hoover Institution Studies 48)

ISBN 0-8447-3145-5
Library of Congress Catalog Card No. 74-29311
4/76

Printed in United States of America

Contents

1

Introduction

In August 1974, Brazil and the People's Republic of China established diplomatic relations.[1] Brazil's decision to recognize Communist China was made by Ernesto Geisel, the fourth army general to become president of Brazil since the overthrow of João Goulart a decade ago.

The new China policy could be simply interpreted as another step in Brazil's march toward major power status. And, in fact, recognition of the People's Republic has become a symbol of Brazilian diplomatic maturity. But more importantly (and immediately), Brazil's move grew out of the ancient Western hope of entering into the fabled China market rather than a quest for grandeur. The emphasis on trade over politics is not surprising, since Brazil's strategy for greatness depends on rapid economic development and that, in turn, depends on a constant expansion of exports.

Whether Brazil will be able to maintain economic growth at the pace of the last half-dozen years is uncertain. In fact, a new conventional wisdom is rapidly developing which asserts the miracle is over. Economists point to Brazil's vastly inflated fuel bill as a severe restraint on its import capacity. In addition, it is sometimes argued that President Geisel is a weak executive, unable to keep even his junior officers in line. Moreover, with floods, a serious meningitis epidemic, and the loss of the world soccer cup, Geisel has been termed an unlucky president— a charge with serious consequences in a culture which stresses the importance of luck over effort in achieving success.[2] The consequences could be serious, because Brazilians do have a habit of not only under-

---

[1] *Jornal do Brasil* (Rio de Janeiro), 16 August 1974, p. 3.

[2] *Latin America* (London), 26 April 1974, pp. 124-125; 2 August 1974, pp. 237-238.

1

rating their leaders, but also themselves, especially after encountering unexpected difficulties.[3]

Despite these problems, however, the author suspects that the Brazilian miracle will continue. The economy, of course, does face difficulties, and they are primarily consequences of the energy crisis. But Brazil could have a viable strategy to overcome that problem. It can draw on its enormous reserves built up over the last few years. After that it can get short-term capital from the developed world. In addition, its financial leaders are working hard to attract Arab petro-dollars—efforts which include Brazil's own sizeable Arab community.[4] Moreover, within five years major investments in its capital goods sector—chemicals, steel, ships, and, recently, aluminum—will begin to pay off, resulting in additional exports and a substantial reduction in imports. Thus, if Brazilians maintain their own self-confidence they should be able to ride out their short-term difficulties and resume their old miracle growth rates in the late 1970s.

Meanwhile, the basic facts about the country continue to be impressive. Its sheer size is well known, but the fact that it has the world's largest untapped hinterland may surprise some. Brazil's population, now probably in excess of 100 million, is increasing at a 2.7 percent annual rate. If the population continues to grow at this rate—which is likely since the government has no plans to institute any kind of official birth control program—it will double by the end of the century.[5]

Brazil's natural resources are phenomenal. (Its only serious problem now is a lack of developed petroleum sources which will make the country vulnerable to rising world oil prices for the next decade.) It has enormous hydroelectric potential, which the Brazilians are cashing in on at a frantic pace. It also has atomic minerals and the beginnings of an ambitious nuclear program, and it possesses the second largest deposit of oil-bearing shale in the world, which is located in the developed, accessible south. In addition, it may have large off-shore deposits

[3] John P. Santos, "A Psychologist Reflects on Brazil and Brazilians," in Eric Baklanoff, ed., *New Perspectives of Brazil* (Nashville, Tenn.: Vanderbilt University Press, 1966), p. 238.

[4] *Wall Street Journal*, 13 August 1974; *O Globo* (Rio de Janeiro), 8 May 1974, p. 18, and *O Globo*, 20 May 1974, p. 18. Recently Brazil received its first Arab loan ($25 million), and it is expected that Brazil's ministers of finance and mines and energy will soon visit Kuwait and Saudi Arabia. *O Estado de São Paulo*, 13 November 1974, p. 17.

[5] *Latin America* (London), 22 February 1974, p. 63.

of oil which the new president, a former chairman of the state oil monopoly, Petrobrás, should be eager to exploit with foreign assistance. In brief, of all the industrialized and semi-industrialized nations, the United States and Brazil may well have the best chance of emerging intact from the energy crisis.

If energy is currently the chief world economic concern, then food must certainly rank as runner-up. But Brazil has little to worry about: it has the world's largest reserve of untapped arable land. More importantly, it is only beginning to undergo the agricultural revolution by adapting technology to its own environmental peculiarities on already cultivated soil. The result has been astonishing increases in soybean, rice, and wheat production. The latter more than tripled between 1967 and 1970.

This abundance has caused problems. For example, the country's internal transportation network (especially the railroads) is woefully inadequate for the job of getting the vast agricultural output to the long-waiting cargo ships. But these bottlenecks can be broken, and the new administration is shifting away from road building in exotic places (such as the Amazon) to overhauling the railroad lines in more productive regions like the state of São Paulo.[6]

Of course, Brazil still has serious economic problems. Even conservative economists are worried about the growing gap between rich and poor. Inflation will certainly pick up this year following worldwide trends. Brazil's fuel bill alone will run around $3 billion in 1974, a sum which represents almost half of her export earnings last year. And most worrisome of all is the coming drop in world trade volume predicted by many. But despite these problems, Brazil is not likely to return to the stagnation of the early 1960s. The country may well continue to grow for some years at a reduced, but respectable, rate, and then begin a fresh burst of "megagrowth."

Politically, the country is more united than ever, and the military seems to be in firm control. The recent succession from President Garrastazú Médici to Ernesto Geisel has been the least traumatic since the 1964 military takeover.

---

[6] The previous administration's plan to open the Amazon for migrants from the impoverished Northeast has been increasingly discredited even by official sources. INCRA, the land reform agency, has recently released a report stating Amazon soils cannot support mass agricultural settlements. The report asserted that, at best, cattle grazing could be supported, and that would require far fewer people than farming. *Latin America* (London), 15 March 1974, p. 83.

Brazil considered by itself is impressive to be sure, but Brazil's potential compared to other major power hopefuls is even more impressive. Japan may have a surging economy, but it is physically small and vulnerable. India has the size and possibly the resources to be a world power, but it is too heterogeneous, and its population too large and too inert. China is admittedly most impressive, but it is easy to exaggerate its economic accomplishments and to minimize its population problem. And there is the great unknown of future internal political troubles. Canada has only size, and Western Europe, for all the regionalists' optimism, remains a collection of very independent nation-states, which, even in cooperative association, remain vulnerable militarily to the Soviet Union and economically to the Arab oil producers.[7] In short, Brazil alone seems to have the requisite size, population, resources, and political stability to be a serious candidate for major power status by the end of the century.

Such a glowing prospect has clearly gone to the heads of some Brazilians. In a recent editorial the publisher of a leading Rio weekly, *Manchete,* boasted: ". . . after the Mirages, in an almost inevitable progression to cover the next decade, there will come Phantoms, modern tanks, Polaris nuclear powered submarines, aircraft carriers, satellites, rockets and the atomic bomb itself."[8] This is a quirky weapons order to say the least, but it is indicative of the new mood in Brazil, and it is worth noting that the magazine has unusually good connections with "official" opinion.

The question for Americans is: What are the opportunities to exploit and the dangers to avoid in dealing with the "new" Brazil? This survey of U.S.-Brazil relations deals with both elements of the question. First, I shall examine how the two nations have treated each other in the past. It is a relationship that stands in sharp contrast to what is normally thought of as United States-Latin American relations. Through circumstance, policy, and luck, each nation has perceived the other not as a threat, but as an economic complement and political ally in the Western Hemisphere. There have been bad moments, of course, and

---

[7] For another analysis of Brazil's chances see Steven L. Spiegel, *Dominance and Diversity* (Boston: Little, Brown, and Co., 1972), p. 103. Spiegel believes two "Middle Powers," India and Brazil, have a chance to attain the status of "Secondary Powers," that is, below the superpowers, but on an equal basis with China, Japan, and the major European states.

[8] Quoted in *Latin American Digest* (Arizona State University), June 1973, p. 7.

strong differences of opinion, but the basic framework of good relations is a sturdy one.

Past performance, however, is no sure guide for the future. Therefore, I shall analyze those men and institutions which will shape the course of Brazilian diplomacy in the coming decades. First, and most broadly, I shall examine the range of opinions contemporary Brazilian intellectuals hold regarding their country's future role in the world and its relationship with the United States. Though opinions obviously vary, there are a surprising number of common assumptions.

Second, I will focus on the two institutions that are the primary molders of Brazilian foreign policy: the foreign ministry, Itamaraty, and the armed forces—or, more specifically, the general staff. The former has long held the dominant position in the shaping and conduct of Brazil's foreign policy, and it has a reputation for professionalism unmatched anywhere in the Brazilian bureaucracy. The latter currently controls the government, and has lately taken an interest in direct involvement in foreign policy formulation rather than simply holding veto power over decisions made by the foreign ministry.

With this as general background, I will turn to several issues that are important in Brazilian-American relations. Brazilians are aware of them, but little consideration has been given these matters in the U.S., even in official circles.

Finally, I will consider the basic issue for the United States in dealing with present-day Brazil: What should our general policy be toward a military-dominated regime? I will offer suggestions for the beginnings of a new policy that will take this problem into account, as well as the opportunities and risks entailed in dealing with an emergent giant.

2

The United States and Brazil:
A Historical Perspective

Students of Brazil once made much of the "independent foreign policy" of former President Jânio Quadros.[1] The thrust of this once flourishing literature can be summarized as follows: (1) Quadros's new policy was a radical departure from past Brazilian policy toward the U.S., and was, therefore, a good thing. (2) The United States had no alternative but to accommodate itself to the new historical epoch.[2]

That this gush of laudatory commentary was more than a little off the mark is borne out by the fact that the "new look" in Brazilian foreign policy died with the Quadros regime, which lasted only seven months. The Quadros policy did not signal a fundamental shift in Brazil's relationship to America and the rest of the world. It had little to do with Brazil's past, present, and future needs. It merely served the immediate purposes of an ambitious, imaginative, insecure, and quixotic politician, who has since slipped into total political obscurity.

From the perspective of the 1970s, the Quadros new look seems an aberration, and a spectacularly brief one at that. But if this "inde-

---

[1] See, for example, Keith Larry Storrs, *Brazil's Independent Foreign Policy, 1961-1964,* Cornell University Latin American Studies Program, Dissertation Series (Ithaca, N. Y.: Cornell University Press, January 1973); John J. Johnson, "Politics and Economics in Brazil," *Current History,* February 1962, especially pp. 90-91; José Honório Rodrigues, "The Foundations of Brazil's Foreign Policy," *International Affairs* (London), July 1962, pp. 324-338. In 1965 a new Brazilian journal, *Política Externa Independente,* was established. It was devoted exclusively to the exegesis of the new policy (which had been changed by then). It lasted three issues.

[2] In case anyone missed the point, the prestigious *Foreign Affairs* published Quadros's "Brazil's New Foreign Policy," in October 1961. Unfortunately for the editors, the author had already left office. More importantly, the analysis and advice offered by the experts and accurately reflected in Quadros's thinking was faulty and of little practical value for Americans and Brazilians.

pendent policy" was a quick detour and not a new direction in Brazilian-American relations, where exactly are the two nations headed? In order to answer that, we must take a look at where they have been. This is not the place for a detailed diplomatic history.[3] Instead, we will consider the development of Brazil's basic interests and where and when these have been compatible or in conflict with American interests.

In general, it is fair to say that the United States and Brazil, through a combination of circumstance, luck, and good policy have maintained comparatively good relations with each other for over 150 years.[4] The relationship has not been without conflict and misunderstanding, but neither has it been marred by chronic cross-purposes and ill-will that has characterized diplomatic intercourse between the U.S. and Argentina and, for that matter, Brazil and Argentina.

The history of relations between the two giants of the Western Hemisphere can be divided into two periods. The first stretches from 1808 to roughly the end of the nineteenth century, and is characterized by the fact that both nations were essentially peripheral to each other's concern. During the second period, the last seventy years, their mutual importance has increased steadily, albeit asymmetrically, with the United States becoming Brazil's *priority* foreign policy problem.

In the first period, there was, of course, contact between the two countries, with some important, though not crucial, decisions being made on both sides. Nevertheless, each country's principal foreign interests were quite different from those of the other. For the United States these interests were, briefly, continental expansion while maintaining the integrity of the union, and staying out of foreign—that is, European—broils.

Unlike the United States, Brazil emerged from its colonial experience a vast continental country, and, therefore, concerned itself with preserving what it already had, rather than expansion. In the course of securing its territorial claims, it fought no less than four wars between 1825 and 1870—against Argentina, Uruguay and Paraguay—and, subsequently, engaged in skillful negotiation with Bolivia, Peru, Vene-

---

[3] For a highly detailed chronology of American-Brazilian relations in the nineteenth century, with a minimum of analysis, see Lawrence F. Hill, *Diplomatic Relations between the United States and Brazil* (Durham, N. C.: Duke University Press, 1932).

[4] The comparison is made explicitly with the other nations of the hemisphere, including Canada, whose relations with us have ranged from outright war to uneasy alliance.

zuela, Great Britain, France and the Netherlands. As a consequence of these efforts, Brazil retained and obtained nearly all it laid claim to.[5]

The British Role

Besides maintaining its territorial integrity, Brazil's only major foreign concern was Great Britain. This grew out of the ancient Anglo-Portuguese alliance, which first became relevant to Brazil in 1808 when the British navy convoyed the Portuguese royal family to the New World and out of the grasp of Napoleon Bonaparte.

When Brazil became independent in 1822, it remained a monarchy, and Britain retained a proprietary interest in the new Brazilian empire. In 1810 the energetic British minister in Rio de Janeiro, Lord Strangford, negotiated a trade treaty that provided for a maximum duty of 15 percent on English goods entering Brazil, while others paid up to 24 percent.[6] The treaty lapsed in 1844, but, by that time, the English were singularly entrenched. They supplied Brazil with most of its import needs, which until 1870 remained largely consumer nondurables (flour, butter, and beer), and then, as the pace of Brazilian industrialization picked up, the British sold a wide variety of capital goods, from textile machinery to coal. They preserved their trade position through ownership of principal export-import firms, banks and insurance companies, steamship lines, railroads, and the telegraph system.[7]

Throughout the nineteenth century, Anglo-Brazilian relations remained difficult. One suspects that the Brazilians, though dependent on the British, no more liked them than did the Americans who, during the same period, also needed British capital and the British navy.[8] The British added to the ill feeling stemming from their economic dominance by intervening in the Argentine-Brazilian war of 1828, forcing a com-

---

[5] Nelson da Sousa Sampio, "The Foreign Policy of Brazil," in Joseph E. Black and Kenneth W. Thompson, eds., *Foreign Policies in a World of Change* (New York: Harper and Row, 1963), pp. 626-627.

[6] This despite the fact that the Portuguese prince regent had two years earlier made Brazilian ports open to all on an equal basis. See Arthur Whitaker, *The United States and the Independence of Latin America, 1808-1830* (Baltimore: Johns Hopkins University Press, 1941), pp. 76-78.

[7] Richard Graham, *Britain and the Onset of Modernization in Brazil, 1850-1914* (London: Cambridge University Press, 1968), pp. 73-111.

[8] Only the French (in 1815) attempted to challenge the British preeminence by making Brazil dependent on France and predominant in South America. See Whitaker, *The United States and the Independence of Latin America*, pp. 204-205.

promise solution which made Uruguay an independent buffer state between the two South American rivals. Since Uruguay had been a province of Brazil from 1821, Brazilian resentment was understandable.[9]

The British further strained relations by mounting a twenty-five year campaign against the slave trade between Africa and Brazil. In 1826, as a quid pro quo for British diplomatic recognition, Brazil agreed to end the slave traffic in three years.

But slavery was vital to the sugar and coffee industry, and the plantation owners (whose support the government desperately needed) assumed—correctly [10]—that this argument was merely the opening shot of a British fight to eradicate Brazilian slavery. So they resisted enforcement of the treaty, and slaves were brought into Brazil at record rates until mid-century.[11] Frustrated, the British Parliament passed the Aberdeen Act of 1845, giving the Admiralty authority to treat all Brazilian slave ships as pirates. In 1850, after failing to stop the slaves on the high seas, the British navy moved into all Brazilian rivers and ports, seizing any vessel capable of transporting human cargo. Within two years the slave trade was nearly finished.[12]

Brazilian-American Relations, 1808–1889

It is clear that Great Britain had the decisive foreign influence on Brazil in the nineteenth century. America played a subordinate, but significant, role, especially in what it chose *not* to do during the years of the Brazilian Empire, 1822–1889.

Thomas Jefferson was first confronted with a major decision about Brazilian-American relations after the Portuguese prince regent, João VI, moved to the New World in 1808. Rather than condemn a revitalized monarchy in the Western Hemisphere or even remain silent,

---

[9] Alan K. Manchester, *British Preeminence in Brazil: Its Rise and Decline* (Chapel Hill, N. C.: University of North Carolina Press, 1933), pp. 155-158.

[10] Graham, *Britain and the Onset of Modernization in Brazil*, pp. 167-171.

[11] José Honório Rodrigues, *Brazil and Africa*, trans. Richard A. Mazzara and Sam Hileman (Berkeley, Calif.: University of California Press, 1965), pp. 159-160.

[12] Graham, *Britain and the Onset of Modernization in Brazil*, pp. 163-166. Brazilian resentment against great power intervention (even for an obviously humanitarian cause) can be found in the writing of a leading Brazilian historian, José Honório Rodrigues. In his *Brazil and Africa*, he characterized British policy as "insolent and offensive," ineffective, often thinly disguised piracy, and rooted in a base desire for gain—that is, to end legitimate Brazilian-African commerce, and secure all the latter's trade for England. Rodrigues, *Brazil and Africa*, pp. 155-173.

Jefferson extended a warm welcome to His Royal Highness and expressed the hope that Brazil "so favored by the gifts of nature, now advanced to a station under your immediate auspices, will find, in the interchange of mutual wants and supplies, the true aliment [sic] of an unchanging friendship with the United States of America." [13] He also took the opportunity to renew formal relations with the Portuguese Court (which had been suspended in 1801 for reasons of economy) by posting a merchant, Henry Hill, as consul to Rio de Janeiro, the first American diplomat in Latin America.[14] Jefferson thus began relations by rejecting an extreme republican policy that would have alienated Brazil for sixty-five years.

James Monroe continued Jefferson's policy, resisting strong pressures to recognize a revolutionary republican regime in the Brazilian state of Pernambuco in 1817. The United States did give (quite properly under international law) belligerency status to the rebels, which made for difficult relations with Rio until the revolt was put down and the matter forgotten.[15]

Monroe faced a more crucial decision five years later, when Dom Pedro I declared Brazil's independence: Should the United States recognize an independent monarchy in the New World, and would such recognition compromise the recently announced Monroe Doctrine? In cabinet discussions, it soon became apparent that only the attorney general, William Wirt, opposed recognition. The others, including that firm antimonarchist, John Quincy Adams, accepted a more narrow and temperate interpretation of the doctrine, despite rumors that the French were using the new regime as a stalking horse for monarchy throughout South America.[16]

---

[13] Letter to the prince regent of Portugal, Washington, 5 May 1808, in *The Life and Selected Writings of Thomas Jefferson,* ed. Adrienne Koch and William Peden (New York: Modern Library, 1944), pp. 587-588.

[14] Hill, *Diplomatic Relations,* pp. 1-2. Consul Hill was in turn warmly received by the prince regent, who promised Americans most-favored-nation status in commerce, freedom of worship, property rights, and equality before Brazilian courts. The British, as we have seen, had other plans regarding trade privileges. Ibid., p. 4.

[15] Ibid., pp. 20-25.

[16] Giving credence to the rumor was the use of French warships in the ending of the republican revolt in Pernambuco. Hill, *Diplomatic Relations,* pp. 28-30. See also Whitaker, *The United States and the Independence of Latin America,* pp. 544-545. John Q. Adams, however, expressed the private hope that a republican Brazil would soon come about, and he predicted the Brazilian-Argentine war would topple the monarchy. Worthington C. Ford, ed., *The Writings of John Quincy Adams* (New York: Macmillan Co., 1917), vol. 7, p. 471.

For its part, Brazil became the only Latin American government to express appreciation and support for the Monroe Doctrine,[17] and its representative in Washington, José Rebello, proposed a treaty of alliance with the U.S. in order to preserve Brazilian independence against Portugal acting alone or in concert with the Holy Alliance. President Monroe rejected this proposal, maintaining a corollary to his policy of noninterference in European affairs, namely, noninterference in disputes between a mother country and its former dependencies.[18]

Although the U.S. followed a prudent course in its general policy toward Brazil,[19] disputes did arise—some of permanent significance. During the War of 1812, the U.S. protested Brazil's failure to prevent British warships from destroying American merchant vessels in Brazilian waters, although Brazil clearly did not possess sufficient sea power to prevent such attacks.[20]

A few years later Brazil complained that Uruguayan privateers which were preying on its merchant marine were being fitted out in Baltimore. The U.S. Congress subsequently passed tighter neutrality legislation, but the privateers were able to skirt the new law with near impunity. In response to further Brazilian protests, Secretary of State John Quincy Adams refused to take direct action, instead referring the matter to the courts.[21]

At approximately the same time, the U.S. protested Brazil's blockade of the La Plata estuary in its war against Argentina in the 1820s. With British support, the Brazilians regularly searched and

---

[17] In 1895, the new senate building in Rio de Janeiro was named the Palácio Monroe, and more importantly, Brazil's most influential foreign minister, Baron Rio-Branco, reiterated his support of the doctrine and used it skillfully against the French and Germans. E. Bradford Burns, *The Unwritten Alliance: Rio-Branco and Brazilian-American Relations* (New York: Columbia University Press, 1966), pp. 146-156.

[18] Hill, *Diplomatic Relations*, p. 31 and Arthur Whitaker, "José Silvestre Rebello: The First Diplomatic Representative of Brazil in the United States," *The Hispanic American Historical Review*, vol. 20 (1940), pp. 380-401. Rebello apparently exceeded instructions in suggesting that the alliance include the Spanish Americans as well—an addition that the imperial court explicitly rejected. Whitaker, "José Silvestre Rebello," pp. 390-391.

[19] This did not mean an official representative of the United States could not commit an occasional republican gaucherie. In 1846 Commodore Rousseau, commander of the American squadron in the South Atlantic, refused to salute the imperial princess's baptism, causing a furor in the Brazilian press. Hill, *Diplomatic Relations*, p. 96.

[20] Ibid., pp. 11-16.

[21] Ibid., pp. 16-20.

seized American blockade runners and impressed their sailors. The matter was not settled until 1830 when the emperor personally intervened by ordering the payment of reparations in thirteen cases.[22]

A far more serious matter to the United States was Brazilian diplomacy during the American Civil War. Brazil adopted precisely the same position the U.S. took during the 1817 Pernambuco revolt, neutrality, which meant it accepted the belligerent status of the Confederacy. In doing so it followed the lead of the European powers. The United States, of course, tried to prevent the Confederacy from obtaining any advantage from a neutral power. But the American chargé in Rio, General J. Watson Webb, was so clumsy that U.S. interests, even in the absence of southern agents in Brazil, were not advanced.[23] Brazilian-American relations thus remained badly strained until well after the war.

More important and more relevant for today was the beginning of the Amazon River controversy.[24] In the mid-nineteenth century, the American hydrographer and astronomer, Lieutenant Matthew Fontaine Maury, USN, argued in a series of articles and lectures that the Amazon basin contained the wealth necessary (through free navigation of the river) to industrialize the American South. On the basis of an analysis of wind direction and ocean currents, Maury announced to readers of *DeBow's Review* that the Amazon "is but a continuation of the Mississippi Valley," and therefore all ships emerging from the river's mouth would be guided by nature to America's southern ports.

Subsequently, an American expedition was formed to descend the Amazon from its Andean headwaters.[25] Brazilian officials did not share Lieutenant Maury's views, and were alarmed by the news of the expedition. They immediately began negotiating treaties with Bolivia and

---

[22] Ibid., pp. 62-63.

[23] Ibid., pp. 146-170. Among Webb's other problems was his credibility. Throughout the war the chargé characterized it as a rebellion that would be quickly crushed.

[24] See below, pp. 96-103.

[25] Quoted in Hill, *Diplomatic Relations,* p. 219. As early as 1825 a group of New York businessmen had negotiated with Brazil's representative, José Rebello, for permission to open up the river to the recently formed New York South American Steamboat Association. The local authorities in Pará, however, refused their permission because they feared some political link existed between the association and republican liberator Simón Bolívar. Whitaker, "José Silvestre Rebello," p. 392.

Peru to exclude Americans from free navigation and trade along the Amazon.[26]

Nearly a half-century later, the matter was still extremely sensitive. In 1899, when an American exploring vessel passed the Amazonian riverport of Manaus, the American consul there was attacked by a mob.[27] The inviolability of the Amazon then became an *idée fixe* for Brazilians, a fact which some Americans would later painfully rediscover.

The American Policy of Rio-Branco

The second broad period of Brazilian-American relations began on 15 November 1889, with the bloodless coup that toppled the empire. In the following decade a series of ad hoc decisions on both sides brought the two nations closer together, in sharp contrast to the growing estrangement between the U.S. and Spanish America. After the turn of the century, this new closeness became the conscious policy of Brazilian statesmen and, to a lesser extent, their American counterparts. The former were quite conscious that Brazil's position in the world was rapidly changing, and that the old policies of balance of power in South America and close ties with England were no longer sufficient.

For the United States, the first step into the new era was recognition of the new republic. The American minister in Rio, Robert Adams, cabled Washington immediately, advising Secretary of State James G. Blaine that the republic was permanent and should be recognized immediately. Blaine was inclined to agree, despite the old emperor's popularity in the United States.[28] Blaine, after receiving heavy criticism from the Democrats for delaying, extended recognition at the end of January 1890.[29] This greatly strengthened the infant republic: the U.S.

---

[26] Hill, *Diplomatic Relations*, pp. 223-224.

[27] Ibid., p. 285.

[28] Telegrams, Robert Adams to James G. Blaine, 16 and 17 November 1889, in *Foreign Relations of the United States, 1889* (Washington, D. C.: Government Printing Office, 1890), p. 59. For a sampling of American opinion on Dom Pedro II, see J. Fred Rippy, "The United States and the Establishment of the Republic of Brazil," *Southwestern Political Science Quarterly,* Fall 1922, pp. 39-53.

[29] Hill, *Diplomatic Relations*, pp. 264-266. Some Democratic newspapers were particularly incensed. The New York *World*, 26 December 1889, wrote that the delay in recognizing the new republic was "cowardly" and then added: "What a sneaking, pottering, cowardly republic we are having under the rule of the Republican plutocracy." And the Indianapolis *Sentinel*, 22 December 1889, thundered: "The attitude of the Government in Washington in this matter is enough to make every patriotic American hang his head with shame. If the Republic of Brazil fails,

was the first major power to extend recognition. This act laid the basis for an exchange of favors that would create the mystique of "traditional" Brazilian-American friendship in the twentieth century.[30]

Brazil reciprocated at the first Pan American Conference by supporting the major proposals of the American delegation: an obligatory arbitration treaty and reciprocal trade agreements. This support was given despite the opposition of a large majority of Spanish-American states led by Chile and Argentina.[31]

Of even greater significance was Brazil's role during the U.S.-Chile crisis of 1891-1892. This crisis climaxed more than a decade of bad Chilean-American relations: In 1881 the United States took it upon itself to attempt to end the War of the Pacific, in which ultimately victorious Chile refused to surrender any territory taken from Peru and Bolivia. In 1890 the U.S. backed the wrong side (the losers) in a Chilean civil war, and in October 1891 sailors from the U.S.S. *Baltimore* were beaten by a Valparaiso waterfront mob. President Benjamin Harrison considered the incident a grave insult to the American uniform and demanded an apology. The Chilean foreign minister replied with even greater belligerence, and by January 1892 Harrison had issued his personal ultimatum to Chile and was drafting a war message for Congress. In the meantime, despite Chile's lengthy campaign to secure Brazilian support, Brazil openly indicated its "friendly neutrality" by decorating Harrison. In addition, Argentina, Peru, and Bolivia, all with old scores to settle with Chile, supported the U.S. Thus, without friends or allies in South America, Chile apologized for the *Baltimore* incident, and the matter was closed.[32]

---

it will be because the United States withholds its recognition.—Oh, for one week of an Andrew Jackson or a Grover Cleveland in the White House!" Quoted in Rippy, "The United States and the Establishment of the Republic of Brazil," pp. 46-47.

[30] The European monarchies slowly accepted the new regime. Russia delayed until six months after the death of Dom Pedro in 1891. Republican France used recognition as a carrot in order to conclude a new border agreement. (The Brazilians refused to bite.) Heitor Lyra, "Europe and the South American Neighbors," in Lawrence Hill, ed., *Brazil* (Berkeley, Calif.: University of California Press, 1947), pp. 326-328.

[31] David S. Muzzey, *James G. Blaine* (New York: Dodd, Mead and Co., 1935), pp. 434-435; Thomas F. McGann, *Argentina, the United States, and the Inter-American System* (Cambridge, Mass.: Harvard University Press, 1957), p. 154.

[32] A. T. Volviler, "Harrison, Blaine, and American Foreign Policy, 1889-1893," *Proceedings of the American Philosophical Society*, vol. 79 (1938), pp. 637-648; Robert Burr, "The Balance of Power in Nineteenth-Century South America: An Exploratory Essay," *Hispanic American Historical Review*, February 1955, p. 56.

The United States, in turn, performed two important services for the young republic. In September 1893, in an attempt to restore the monarchy, the navy revolted in Rio harbor. Despite the support the revolt had in the Brazilian southern states and the covert sympathy of European powers, President Grover Cleveland refused to give the rebels belligerent status. Furthermore, the American squadron at Rio placed itself athwart the Brazilian navy's line of fire, permitting the government to reinforce its position with a steady stream of supplies.[33] The checkmated insurgents finally surrendered in March 1894. The Brazilian Congress promptly awarded Cleveland a medal, and the following Fourth of July was observed as an official Brazilian holiday.[34]

Grover Cleveland received another Brazilian tribute the following year when, as official arbiter, he decided in favor of Brazil in a territorial dispute with Argentina. The award granted Brazil nearly 14,000 square miles, thanks in large part to Baron Rio-Branco's brief, which Cleveland studied with great care.[35]

During the Spanish-American War, Brazil was the only Latin American country to maintain a friendly—toward the U.S.—neutrality. Two examples of Brazilian actions clearly demonstrate that the emphasis was on "friendly": three warships were sold to the United States, and on one occasion two American warships were permitted to remain in Brazilian waters longer than the rules of neutrality allowed.[36]

By the turn of the century, both America and Brazil had changed enormously. The U.S. had completed its continental expansion, and had acquired Alaska, Hawaii, Puerto Rico, and the Philippines. Internal unity was assured, industrialization was well along after a generation of feverish expansion, and the nation's elite was becoming quite conscious of America's emerging world role.

Brazil was a secure republic with its immense territory intact. Border agreements had been signed or were on the verge of completion with all neighboring countries, and in only one case did Brazil receive

---

[33] In frustration, one rebel vessel fired a shot at the U.S.S. *Detroit*. *Detroit* refused to move, and returned the compliment by firing a six-pounder, with the shell falling short in the water. Hill, *Diplomatic Relations,* pp. 278-279.

[34] Ibid., pp. 273-281.

[35] A city in the state of Paraná was renamed Clevelândia in honor of the American President.

[36] At the end of the war, the Clube Naval wired congratulations to the U.S. Navy for its brilliant victories. Hill, *Diplomatic Relations,* p. 284; Burns, *The Unwritten Alliance,* p. 61.

less than expected.[37] Although relations with Argentina were hardly cordial, that nation, even with allies, could no longer threaten Brazil's national security. Industrialization had begun, and although well behind that in the U.S., this process would heavily influence the nation's diplomacy. Finally, Brazil's trade patterns had changed substantially: not only were its imports shifting away from consumer to capital goods, but, more importantly, its exports were no longer going principally to Europe. In 1865, the United States had become the chief consumer of Brazil's most important product: coffee.[38] By 1912, the U.S. was purchasing 36 percent of Brazil's total coffee production.[39]

The foreign minister who took office in 1902, José María da Silva Paranhos, the Baron Rio-Branco, fully appreciated Brazil's changing world position. After taking office as foreign minister, he publicly observed that "Washington is our most important post." [40]

As Brazilian consul in commercial Liverpool for fifteen years, he had acquired a thorough working knowledge of international economics, and he vigorously defended free entry into the American market. When the gap between U.S. purchases of Brazilian goods and Brazil's imports of American products increased 60 percent in eight years (1902–1910), he attempted to reduce the high Brazilian tariff wall.[41]

Rio-Branco saw great political advantages in a tacit alliance with the United States: As America's only close friend in the hemisphere, Brazil could count on American support in any dispute with a South American neighbor and, perhaps, European powers as well. In pursuing that alliance, Rio-Branco publicly and repeatedly endorsed the Monroe Doctrine, something which no Spanish-American statesman had dared to do.

---

[37] This was thanks to the arbitration of the Italian king, who awarded more territory to the British than they had even claimed. Lyra, "Europe and the South American Neighbors," pp. 333-334; Burns, *The Unwritten Alliance*, pp. 47-48.

[38] Brazilian diplomats from the 1880s to World War I successfully fought off numerous attempts of the American Congress to place a duty on coffee, even in retaliation for the Brazilian export tax on the product. Ambassador Joaquim Nabuco was perhaps the most successful, since his friends included the most powerful men in Washington. Burns, *The Unwritten Alliance*, pp. 63-67.

[39] Ibid., pp. 63-64. In the meantime, Spanish-American purchases remained negligible.

[40] Ibid., p. 161.

[41] His efforts with the Brazilian Congress were finally successful in 1906, but exports did not increase greatly until World War I. Ibid., pp. 68-75.

He also used the doctrine to Brazil's advantage in a dispute with Bolivia over Acre, a remote but valuable piece of territory in the Amazon basin. In 1900 Bolivia exercised nominal jurisdiction over Acre, though Brazil and Peru had claims on it too, and though the majority of the population was Brazilian. In a desperate attempt to maintain control of the area, Bolivia virtually agreed to turn over Acre to the Bolivian Syndicate, a mixed group of American and European investors. It was Bolivia's clear intention to garner official U.S. support for its claim through the latter's interest in the protection of American investment.

Rio-Branco, fully aware of these plans, rejected a frontal attack on the U.S. and instead successfully persuaded the State Department that European investments in South America constituted a potential violation of the Monroe Doctrine.[42] The syndicate, having lost any chance of official American protection, sold its interests to Brazil, and Acre was annexed after final negotiations with Bolivia in 1903.[43]

Rio-Branco further distinguished Brazil from the rest of Latin America by strongly supporting the American position on Panamanian independence and endorsing the Roosevelt Corollary to the Monroe Doctrine. That famous corollary announced America's intention to intervene in the internal affairs of those Latin American states that refused to meet their international obligations, thus inviting European meddling if not outright occupation. Brazil, its foreign minister argued, had no need for concern, nor did any other state that acted responsibly. Furthermore, he engaged in preliminary talks with Argentina and Chile on an agreement that would provide for similar intervention in case such problems arose among their smaller, more turbulent neighbors.[44] In a wider arena, Rio-Branco criticized the extreme nonintervention doctrine advanced by Spanish America at every inter-American gathering for decades, a doctrine first articulated by Argentine Foreign Minister Luis Drago in 1902.[45]

As another part of Rio-Branco's policy of creating a unique role for Brazil in the hemisphere, he offered his country's services to the United States as mediator and interpreter of Latin America. He argued

---

[42] This, of course, did not discourage Rio-Branco from convincing European investors to stay out of the syndicate, a tactic that worked at least in the case of Germany. Ibid., p. 80.

[43] Ibid., pp. 76-86; Hill, *Diplomatic Relations,* pp. 285-291.

[44] Burns, *The Unwritten Alliance,* pp. 151-153.

[45] Arthur Whitaker, *The Western Hemisphere Idea* (Ithaca, N. Y.: Cornell University Press, 1954), pp. 87-89 and pp. 95-107.

that while Brazil, like America, remained apart from the rest of the hemisphere, Brazil was more aware of Spanish America's problems and sensitivities. Rio-Branco proved his point by successfully mediating a dispute between the U.S. and Chile in 1909, and, three years earlier, preventing an American blunder by warning Secretary of State Elihu Root that his arbitration scheme, to be proposed at a forthcoming Pan American Conference, would be totally abhorrent to Chile.[46]

Rio-Branco succeeded in establishing a special relationship with the United States, and used it to Brazil's advantage in preserving its markets in North America and settling territorial disputes with Spanish-American and European states. In the latter instances, with the support of the United States (or, at least, the illusion of American support), Brazil nearly always emerged the victor.

That Rio-Branco's friendship for the United States was rooted in self-interest—that, in fact, he was an ardent nationalist—is amply demonstrated by his chronic suspicion of any American interest in the Amazon. According to the American authority on Rio-Branco, he had a "nagging distrust of North American intentions toward the Amazon." [47] He not only was determined to keep U.S. private interests out of Acre, he even viewed with considerable suspicion the trip up river of a group of American tourists in 1909.[48]

He was capable of opposing U.S. policy, as he did at the second Hague Peace Conference when he argued for equality of representation on the proposed arbitration court rather than having the selection of judges limited to the larger states as called for in the American plan.[49]

Rio-Branco's casting a new role for Brazil as the second major power in the hemisphere—the South American twin of the North American giant—was apparently accepted by the United States. As one student of Brazilian-American relations observed: "The United States seemed willing to acknowledge Brazil's preeminence in South America. No evidence exists that any United States official tried to deride Brazil's ambitions. To the contrary, several high officials encouraged Itamaraty's aspirations." [50] In fact, Brazil's greatness was one of Theodore Roose-

[46] Burns, *The Unwritten Alliance,* p. 175.
[47] Ibid., p. 178.
[48] Ibid., pp. 178-179.
[49] Ibid., pp. 116-131.
[50] Ibid., p. 173.

velt's favorite themes, a sharp contrast to his well-known contempt for the smaller, more turbulent Spanish-American republics.[51]

Rio-Branco remained foreign minister until his death in 1912, and his prestige was so enormous that his policies, especially the carefully constructed relationship with the United States, remained sacrosanct for a half-century.[52]

After Rio-Branco's death, Brazilian statesmen did little but adjust the old policy to fit new situations. For example, in 1914 Brazil, together with Argentina and Chile, offered to mediate between the United States and Mexico. Woodrow Wilson, who had misjudged the Mexican reaction to his ordered occupation of Veracruz, quickly and gladly accepted. Meanwhile, all over Latin America—except in Brazil—riots and demonstrations broke out against the American intervention.[53] After U.S.-Mexico relations were broken as a result of Veracruz, Brazil handled American business in Mexico and Brazilian diplomat J. M. Cardoso de Oliveira became Washington's prime source of information on conditions in Mexico City.[54]

Brazil also continued to side with the United States on the issue of nonintervention. At the 1928 Pan American Conference in Havana, for example, the Brazilians vigorously argued against the Drago Doctrine and for international responsibility, while the U.S. played a far more subdued role.

Brazil may well have moved beyond its immediate interest in preserving the special relationship with the United States during World War I. It remained neutral when America was neutral, then, less than

---

[51] Ibid., pp. 97, 100, 114, and 173. In this he was more than matched by Rio-Branco himself, who distrusted Spanish Americans and found, for example, the Peruvians to be a "very false and pretentious people." Quoted in ibid., p. 168.

[52] To further insure his influence, Rio-Branco also reformed the foreign ministry, Itamaraty. He increased the size of the professional staff, organized the library and archives, and attracted able men by good salaries and his own fame. By 1912, the foreign service had become the most professional and efficient in South America —and probably the entire hemisphere—and its prestige would become as great as its founder. Ibid., pp. 38-40.

[53] Arthur Link, *Woodrow Wilson: The New Freedom* (Princeton, N. J.: Princeton University Press, 1956), pp. 401-407. At the beginning of his administration, Wilson had earned Brazil's favor by dropping a Justice Department suit begun in the Taft administration against a coffee price-fixing scheme drawn up by American coffee merchants and the Brazilian government. The details are in Leon F. Sensabaugh, "The Coffee-Trust Question in United States-Brazilian Relations: 1912-1913," *Hispanic American Historical Review*, vol. 26 (1946), pp. 480-496.

[54] Arthur Link, *Woodrow Wilson: The Struggle for Neutrality* (Princeton, N. J.: Princeton University Press, 1960), p. 460.

two months after the United States declared war on the Central Powers, Brazil revoked her neutrality decree (relations with Germany had been severed in April 1917) and, in October 1917, declared war—although the only *casus belli* was the sinking of a lone Brazilian freighter in 1917.[55]

Brazil, however, did feel free to act on her own as an incipient major power when American interests were not involved. Thus, at the League of Nations, it persistently lobbied for a permanent seat on the council, arguing that the Western Hemisphere needed ongoing representation by a large power. The argument convinced few in Geneva, and Brazil withdrew from the League in 1926.[56]

Despite this Brazilian-American closeness, however, there were difficulties between the two nations, especially after the onset of the depression with all of its international dislocations. Brazil suspended debt payments on several occasions, which provoked protest in the United States and Europe. The Brazilian military was angered by a Brazilian-American debt payment accord that called for cuts in Brazil's national budget, and, in 1937, the military was further angered when the United States was persuaded by Argentina not to sell three destroyers to Brazil's navy.[57]

On the other hand, Brazilian and American diplomats kept the special friendship alive in the wake of Getúlio Vargas's November 1937 coup, which provoked strong criticism in the United States, principally from the *New York Times* and Senator William Borah. In Washington, Brazilian ambassador Oswaldo Aranha, after overcoming his own uncertainty about Vargas's move, exploited his close friendship with Assistant Secretary of State Sumner Welles, persuading him not to act against the new regime. Three weeks later, Welles publicly praised Vargas and berated the regime's American critics.[58]

Immediately after the coup, the Brazilian foreign minister, and then Vargas himself, consulted Jefferson Caffrey, the American ambassador to Rio, explaining the reasons behind the coup and requesting American support. Caffrey was a close personal friend of Vargas and

---

[55] Hill, *Diplomatic Relations*, pp. 302-303.

[56] Lyra, "Europe and the South American Neighbors," p. 340.

[57] Robert M. Levine, *The Vargas Regime: The Critical Years, 1934-1938* (New York: Columbia University Press, 1970), pp. 40, 157, and 170.

[58] Ibid., p. 153.

did not urge strong American reaction, though he had few illusions about the nature of what Getúlio Vargas would call the Estado Nôvo.[59]

The Wartime Alliance

The growing strength of Nazi Germany confronted Brazil with a difficult choice: It could remain at the side of the U.S. and the European democracies or it could assume a neutral stance. Vargas chose a cautious approach—at least before December 1941. On the one hand, he privately assured Americans of his basic sympathy for hemispheric solidarity and democracy, and he very carefully controlled the strength of Brazil's indigenous, self-consciously fascist movement, Integralismo—never showing the enthusiasm for fascism that a number of other South American regimes did before and during the war. But on the other hand, Vargas made public statements respecting those "vigorous peoples" who were doing away with the old and building the new. "The era of improvident liberalism, sterile demagoguery, useless individualism, and disorder has passed," he stated to Brazilian military officers.[60] In the meantime, the army continued to be supplied with German arms (although the French had the largest military mission) and the German embassy carried on a vigorous propaganda campaign from São Paulo.[61]

As the American perception of the German threat grew, Brazilian-American relations took another turn—this time for the worse. The American military wanted to station U.S. troops in the strategically important Brazilian Northeast, the New World's shortest route to German-occupied West Africa. The Brazilians repeatedly refused permission and insisted on defending their own soil themselves, albeit with generous American arms assistance. Unfortunately, despite repeated Brazilian demands and subsequent American promises, American arms aid was not available, as the United States was desperately late in its defense-preparedness program.

A joint agreement to build a steel plant (a favorite project of Vargas) kept relations from seriously deteriorating, but only after Pearl Harbor were solid defense commitments made, forging the wartime

---

[59] Ibid., pp. 150 and 153. See also John W. F. Dulles, *Vargas of Brazil: A Political Biography* (Austin: University of Texas Press, 1967), pp. 173-174, 181, and 192-193.

[60] Quotes in Dulles, *Vargas of Brazil*, p. 210.

[61] Ibid., p. 212.

alliance. The U.S. dropped its insistence on stationing troops and rearranged the Munitions Allocations Board priorities to meet Brazil's need for weapons. The Brazilians, for their part, provided naval and air bases in the Northeast and granted permission to station the large contingent of U.S. maintenance personnel required to assure the smooth functioning of the air bridge between Brazil and Africa. In January 1942 the careful Brazilian neutrality of the 1930s was completely set aside with the breaking of diplomatic and commercial relations with the Axis countries.[62] In the seven months following the break in relations, fourteen Brazilian ships were torpedoed, leading to a declaration of war against Germany and Italy in August 1942.

Vargas and the military were not satisfied, however, with the simple, passive role of supplying bases and strategic minerals for the United States. They wished to send troops to Europe, and after some U.S. Army hesitation, the offer was accepted by General George C. Marshall. The Brazilian Expeditionary Force (FEB), with an air detachment, was assigned to the Italian front, fought well, and had the distinction of receiving the first surrender of a German division in Italy.[63] The United States and Brazil, for the first time in their histories, had become working military allies. This cooperation would have an effect far beyond the end of the war.[64]

After the war, the U.S. attempted to continue the close relationship by completing the Volta Redonda steel mill and by urging a permanent seat for Brazil on the United Nations Security Council (the U.S.S.R. vetoed it).[65] But close, personal collaboration between the two countries was difficult. Roosevelt—who had liked the Brazilians—was dead; Getúlio Vargas had been in power for fifteen years, and pressures were mounting for him to resign. In 1945, the premature praise by the new American ambassador, Adolph Berle, for Vargas's "promise" to hold elections angered Vargas (and, much later, left-wing nationalists), but

[62] Ibid., pp. 221-227. Thomas E. Skidmore, *Politics in Brazil: 1930-1964* (New York: Oxford University Press, 1967), pp. 44-45.

[63] Alfred Stepan, *The Military in Politics: Changing Patterns in Brazil* (Princeton, N. J.: Princeton University Press, 1971), pp. 128-129 and 174-178. See also Dulles, *Vargas of Brazil*, pp. 239-241.

[64] See below, pp. 80-82.

[65] Werner Baer, *The Development of the Brazilian Steel Industry* (Nashville: Vanderbilt University Press, 1969), pp. 75-79. See also Dulles, *Vargas of Brazil*, p. 345.

placed the dictator in an untenable position. A month later, he resigned at the insistence of the military.[66]

Vargas's dictatorship was over, and the Brazilian-American alliance, while not at an end, would nevertheless undergo changes that removed it from the Rio-Branco design. It was not replaced by an equally clear or consistent set of policies, however.

Little change was apparent at first. The administration of General Eurico Dutra continued the policy of close cooperation with the U.S., and, if anything, was more anti-Communist than its wartime ally. In 1947, for example, Brazil broke diplomatic relations with the Soviet Union and at the Western Hemisphere conference that drew up the Inter-American Treaty for Reciprocal Assistance, Brazil supported the American position for a strong political collective security agreement against the Argentines, the Guatemalans, and Cubans, among others. The United States in exchange agreed to a joint economic commission unique in Latin America that would study Brazil's development needs and propose a detailed loan program.[67]

By mid-century, the U.S. and Brazil had reached the zenith of their relationship. For the United States, Brazil had been the most important Latin American military ally during World War II. Brazil was also the single consistently reliable U.S. political partner in the region. For Brazil, America had become its leading market, its leading source for foreign investment and public capital, its prime supplier of arms, and the model for the organization of its armed forces. But this very closeness—indeed, dependence—which had grown out of the depression and the war carried within it the seeds of its own destruction.

In 1950, Getúlio Vargas returned to the presidency. But even his return could not stem the decline of the old-time collaboration. The U.S. was occupied with rebuilding Europe and the struggle in Korea. An indirect casualty of the Korean War was the loan program drawn up by the joint Brazilian-American commission. Only half the planned projects were funded, to Brazil's disappointment. The fact that the rest of Latin America received far less attention did little to mollify Vargas.[68]

On the other hand, despite growing leftist-nationalist clamor, Vargas pursued a middle course on foreign investment, imposing restrictions on profit remittances, but avoiding more extreme measures. In

---

[66] Dulles, *Vargas of Brazil*, pp. 269-274; Skidmore, *Politics in Brazil*, p. 51.
[67] Dulles, *Vargas of Brazil*, p. 304.
[68] Ibid., pp. 310-312.

addition, he made petroleum production a state monopoly, but put the state agency, Petrobrás, in the charge of a nonnationalist, Juracy Magalhães.[69]

Within the armed forces, changes were taking place that would affect the future course of U.S.-Brazil relations. A group of nationalist—and generally leftist—officers who had not served in Europe became more outspoken with the support of Vargas's war minister, Newton Estilac Leal. Their influence helped dissuade Vargas from honoring the specific request of the United States that he send troops to Korea. One nationalist officer, anonymously, contributed an article to a military journal accusing the U.S. of aggression against North Korea.[70] The ensuing uproar over the contribution of "Capitão X" to the pages of *A Revista do Clube Militar* polarized the army into factions that would openly vie for power within the armed forces command until the 1964 revolution.[71]

After Vargas's suicide death in August 1954, anti-American nationalists gained further strength with the publication of his self-serving suicide note [72] which alluded to the machinations of "international economic and financial groups." [73] Vargas's elected successor, Juscelino Kubitschek, sought to accommodate the nationalists by promoting a highly nationalistic development program and maintaining a certain distance from the United States.

Kubitschek pursued a course similar to that of Vargas. On the one hand, he encouraged foreign investment, especially in manufacturing,[74] and, on the other, he defended Petrobrás, denounced the International Monetary Fund, and, after a highly vocal campaign conducted by the nationalists, slowed down export of radioactive minerals to the United States. In addition, he reestablished trade contacts with the Communist bloc and, in 1960, took it upon himself to attempt mediation of the U.S.-Cuba dispute. But Kubitschek's most spectacular display

---

[69] Ibid., pp. 309-313; Skidmore, *Politics in Brazil,* pp. 96-99.

[70] Skidmore, *Politics in Brazil,* p. 105; Dulles, *Vargas of Brazil,* p. 334.

[71] Skidmore, *Politics in Brazil,* pp. 105-107.

[72] The note was self-serving, because up to the moment of his death, Vargas was in a difficult political position. Two weeks earlier, members of his personal guard had arranged the assassination of the regime's most consistent critic, Carlos Lacerda, but had failed, killing an air force major instead. Ibid., p. 138.

[73] Dulles, *Vargas of Brazil,* p. 334.

[74] As the steel plant became Vargas's pet project, the automobile industry became Kubitschek's.

of independence was the unveiling of "Operação Pan-Americana," which criticized the U.S. for its "neglect" of Latin America and proposed a costly, multilateral socioeconomic uplift venture for the Western Hemisphere. At the same time, Kubitschek made favorable references to the Monroe Doctrine (probably the last heard in Brazil) and unfavorable ones to communism.[75]

Brazil's Independent Foreign Policy and After

Having legitimized overt presidential criticism of the United States, the cautious Kubitschek prepared the way for Quadros's full-blown reaction to Brazil's special dependence on the U.S. In 1960, campaigning as a fiscal conservative, Quadros attracted the nationalist vote with the promise of a new and independent foreign policy. This policy consisted of a series of gestures rather than programs, but each became a symbol of Brazil's independence from the United States: Quadros's refusal to visit the U.S. before inauguration, his highly publicized argument with Adolph Berle, his initiation of informal talks with the East Germans (which Itamaraty[76] promptly repudiated), and his decoration of Dr. Ernesto "Che" Guevara with Brazil's highest medal, the Cruzeiro do Sul.[77]

As for substance, Quadros argued that Brazil needed to assert itself, and could do so by finding new markets in the Third World (principally in Africa) and mediating between the cold-war contenders. That Africa was more competitor than market, that both the United States and the Soviet Union were quite capable of negotiating without the assistance of outsiders, and that racial similarities open no doors apparently escaped Quadros's notice. Yet for the United States, the old relationship had ended, and an uncomfortable, undefined one had taken its place.

---

[75] Victor Wallis, "Brazil's Experiment with an Independent Foreign Policy," in Yale H. Ferguson, ed., *Contemporary Inter-American Relations* (Englewood Cliffs, N. J.: Prentice-Hall, 1972), p. 43.

[76] The foreign ministry's semi-official name "Itamaraty" is derived from its former headquarters in downtown Rio de Janeiro, the Palacio Itamaraty, formerly owned by the Baron of Itamaraty. The new foreign ministry building in Brasilia is also called Itamaraty while the old headquarters in Rio has been given to the Rio-Branco Institute, the two year preparatory school for young diplomats.

[77] See Quadros's *Foreign Affairs* article reprinted in Carlos A. Astiz, ed., *Latin American International Politics: Ambitions, Capabilities and the National Interest of Mexico, Argentina and Brazil* (Notre Dame, Ind.: Notre Dame Press, 1969), pp. 248-258.

The Goulart years were also difficult, but new issues arose. The independent foreign policy was continued, but the government was chiefly concerned with Brazil's growing domestic problems, principally inflation. Goulart made no showy Quadros-style gestures, and he even attempted to cooperate with the U.S. to the extent of acquiring fresh credits to pay off old and due debts. Friction did develop over (largely threatened) nationalizations of American-owned public utilities, but this was not so much Goulart's doing as it was Leonel Brizzola's, Goulart's demagogic brother-in-law and governor of Rio Grande do Sul.

In the meantime, diplomatic relations with the Soviet Union were renewed cautiously, but Brazilian enthusiasm for Third World leadership dimmed somewhat. The only serious clash between the United States and Brazil on a strictly foreign policy issue was Cuba. After 1960, the U.S. argued that Fidel Castro was a threat to the hemisphere's security, while Brazil resisted attempts at collective action. (During the October 1962 missile crisis, however, it did support the naval blockade.)

The independent foreign policy, in any real sense, did not survive the 1964 revolution. In fact, for a brief period, the old wartime relationship seemed to blossom again. The new Brazilian chief executive, General Humberto Castelo Branco, a member of the World War II Brazilian Expeditionary Force, felt Brazil was an integral member of the Western alliance and the United States was, in the words of the new foreign minister, Juracy Magalhães, the "unquestioned leader of the free world." [78]

To prove its commitment to the Western alliance, Brazil promptly broke relations with Cuba, sent troops to the Dominican Republic, and promised help if the Vietnam War became worldwide in scope.[79]

These policies were rooted in conviction, not expedience. America's response was overwhelming—not only was quick recognition granted, but a billion dollars of aid designed to bail out the floundering Brazilian economy was either hurriedly disbursed or freshly appropriated. But this new intimacy also proved ephemeral, since it was based, in large part, on the close working relationship of three men: President Castelo Branco, U.S. military attaché, General Vernon Walters (who had served as liaison officer between the U.S. Fifth Army and the Brazilian Expedi-

---

[78] Peter D. Bell, "Brazilian-American Relations," in Riordan Roett, ed., *Brazil in the Sixties* (Nashville, Tenn.: Vanderbilt University Press, 1972), p. 93.
[79] Ibid.

tionary Force during World War II), and the American ambassador, Dr. Lincoln Gordon.

General Artur da Costa e Silva, who succeeded Castelo Branco in 1967, had not served in the FEB. And furthermore, younger, non-FEB officers were beginning to espouse nationalist, although non-leftist, positions. In pointed fashion, Costa e Silva withdrew support from the Inter-American Peace Force in the Dominican Republic, demanded U.S. trade concessions, and complained about insufficient military aid.[80]

At the same time, the new American ambassador, John Tuthill, had no longstanding interest in Brazil, and felt the U.S. had become over-committed as the result of the intimate, unprofessional relationship that had developed between Castelo Branco and Tuthill's predecessor, Ambassador Lincoln Gordon. Moreover, the tightening control of the regime plus worldwide publicity about torture of political prisoners moved Tuthill to push for a lower-profile policy toward Brazil by cutting sharply into the size of the embassy staff and the aid program.[81]

The desire to lessen Brazil's dependence on the U.S. seemed mutual. The Brazilians were looking for new markets with much greater skill and aggressiveness than ever before, new sources of foreign capital were being wooed (principally from Japan), and European arms were again being purchased. Anti-Americanism was no longer a substitute for foreign policy, but Brazil and the United States were moving uneasily away from the relationship that had evolved in the 1930s and 1940s.

---

[80] Ibid., pp. 97-98.
[81] John Tuthill, "Operation Topsy," *Foreign Policy,* Fall 1972, pp. 62-85.

3

Brazilian Intellectuals
and Foreign Policy

Among the key variables that will influence Brazilian-American relations is how and what Brazilians are thinking about their country's future in the world, especially its relationship to the United States. On what do they agree, and when they disagree, who will prevail? What possibilities have they included in their thinking, and which, no matter how plausible to the outsider, have they ruled out? And finally, precisely who are *they*?

We shall proceed by answering the last first. Broadly speaking, "they" are the intellectuals, the intelligentsia, the thinkers, "the scribbling set," in Joseph Schumpeter's phrase, who "wield the power of the spoken and the written word." [1]

Merely because they work with their minds and their thoughts are transmitted to a wide audience does not mean, necessarily, that the quality of the product is high. It may well be, as Raymond Aron has said of French intellectuals, that their opinions are quite similar to non-intellectuals at first impression since they have the same mixture of "half-baked knowledge, of traditional prejudices, of preferences which are more aesthetic than rational, as . . . those of shopkeepers or industrialists." [2] In short, intellectuals are defined here by the salable product of their minds—words and ideas—but not by any inherent quality of that product.

---

[1] Joseph Schumpeter, *Capitalism, Socialism and Democracy* (New York: Harper and Row, Harper Torchbooks, 1962), p. 147. Schumpeter also includes a further characteristic: the "absence of direct responsibility for practical affairs," which is only partly true for Brazilian intellectuals. Ibid.

[2] Raymond Aron, *The Opium of the Intellectuals*, trans. Terence Kilmartin (New York: Doubleday, 1957), p. 213.

Brazilian intellectuals who are professionally interested in foreign policy only recently have made an appearance in any number. Before 1955 only an occasional book appeared,[3] usually a gracefully written collection of essays or speeches on Brazilian-Portuguese friendship[4] or on inter-American solidarity.[5] These were customarily written by men who were or had been with the foreign ministry. After 1955, there was an explosion of books, journals and newspaper articles devoted to some aspect of foreign policy. Over seventy-five volumes devoted in whole or in part to Brazil's foreign policies were published between 1955 and 1970. In addition, a number of journals slanted to international topics have come on the scene. At least a half dozen have popped up.

Another recent development has been the creation of institutes of foreign area and policy research. The Instituto Superior de Estudos Brasileiros, set up within the Ministry of Education in 1955 (but dissolved in 1964), devoted itself to constructing a nationalist foreign policy. The Instituto Brasileiro de Relações Internacionais (founded in 1956) maintains a library and publishes the *Revista Brasileira de Política Internacional*. In 1961, Jânio Quadros decreed the founding of an Institute of Afro-Asian studies. Finally, the Escola Superior de Guerra (ESG), organized in 1950, has trained both military officers and civilians in the art of thinking systematically about problems in national security.

Because foreign policy has only recently become popular among intellectuals, a generation of specialists has not been trained.[6] Writers on foreign affairs have included not only historians and economists, but literary critics, novelists, and even a musicologist.

---

[3] Eduardo Prado's polemic, *A Ilusão Americana,* first published and suppressed in 1893, was a rare exception, and even his work was more of a critique of U.S.-Brazilian relations (actually, relations with *any* American republic—Prado was a staunch monarchist) than a series of proposals for a new Brazilian foreign policy. But the book is still popular in Brazil. Eduardo Prado, *A Ilusão Americana,* 3rd ed. (São Paulo: Editôra Brasiliense Ltda., 1961).

[4] João Neves da Fontoura, *Palavras aos Portugueses* (Rio de Janeiro: Edições Dois Mundos, 1946), and Pizarro Loureiro, *Getúlio Vargas e a Política Luso-Brasileira* (Rio de Janeiro: Zélio Valverde-Editor, 1941).

[5] Alfonso de Toledo Bandeira de Melo, *O Espírito do Pan Americanismo* (Rio de Janeiro: Ministério das Relações Exteriores, 1956), and José Carlos do Macedo Soares, *Conceitos da Solidaridade Continental* (Rio de Janeiro: Ministério das Relações Exteriores, 1959).

[6] The foreign ministry does provide its incoming officers two years of training at the Rio-Branco Institute, which helps explain its continued hold on foreign policy making. See below, pp. 70-71.

A striking characteristic of intellectuals in Brazil is that they do not do, at least to the same degree, what their counterparts in other countries do, that is, they do not produce ideas from which policy makers may select.[7] In Brazil, during recent decades, the order has usually been reversed: a popular political leader selects the themes, and the intellectuals expand and refine them, but never alter the basic discussion guidelines. This process continues until another politician suggests new themes for discussion.[8]

In the 1950s, Getúlio Vargas began promoting economic nationalism and sparked a furious debate on one aspect of foreign policy: foreign investment.[9] The issue was most prominent in the presidential campaign of 1950, and the principal target was the largely American-owned mining industry.[10] In the five years following Vargas's death the overwhelming majority of Brazilian works on foreign policy concerned these themes, especially the problem of the state oil monopoly, Petrobrás. From 1954 to 1968, at least thirty books and sixty-five journal articles appeared on the subject of foreign investment.

Thus, when Vargas promoted economic nationalism, the intellectuals followed his lead. Beginning with the 1960 presidential campaign, a similar scene was acted out between candidate Jânio Quadros and the intelligentsia. But the themes were different.

The Quadros initiatives emphasized winning new friends in Africa and Asia, and included hints about Brazil's leadership of this vast area.

---

[7] C. E. Black, *The Dynamics of Modernization* (New York: Harper and Row, 1966), p. 63, and Schumpeter, *Capitalism*, p. 147. This is not true for Brazilian military intellectuals, who have gravitated toward the general staff and its command school and whose work has shaped the thinking of a significant part of the armed forces.

[8] There is, of course, the feedback effect: intellectuals can create a climate of opinion which may well affect future decision makers. Indeed, they may provide the necessary expertise to complete a Frankenstein monster that could turn on its creator.

[9] Arthur P. Whitaker and David C. Jordan, *Nationalism in Contemporary Latin America* (New York: Free Press, 1966), pp. 81-83.

[10] Curiously, the intellectuals did not pick up a neutralist theme that Vargas outlined in September 1950. He said: "To cooperate in a system tending to balance the forces of the militarily weaker countries with the two major powers that history has known—here is the gigantic task that is incumbent on the diplomacy of all nations." He continued: "the existence of such great risks and the extensive identity of interests ought to carry the non-militarized countries to a solid and indestructible union. Only with the formation of a nucleus of nations, powerful and cohesive, will we be sure that we will receive respect for our rights always.... The moment to launch the bases for this balancing force is the present." From a speech in Niteroi, 3 September 1950. Getúlio Vargas, *A Companha Presidencial* (São Paulo: Livraria José Olýmpio, 1951), p. 299.

"The general lines of Brazilian diplomacy follow Victorian molds," argued Quadros, adding, ". . . we ought to be more dynamic." [11]

Quadros endlessly repeated these themes during and after the campaign. As a result, the focus of attention shifted away from the *getulista* subjects. The literature on investment dropped sharply, but the 1960 to 1965 period produced at least twenty books and a dozen journal articles by Brazilians on Afro-Asian relations. In the previous decade there had been only two books and no articles devoted to the subject. [12] It seems clear that Brazilian intellectuals are commentators rather than innovators. This does not mean they are without importance. In the first place, there is the "feedback effect." A political leader may become the prisoner of his ideas as a result of their having acquired a powerful constituency through the work of the scribblers. Second, while the politician may set the stage initially, the intellectuals may feel perfectly free to move the furniture about as they please before, during, and after the performance. To change the metaphor, the ideas may be debated, criticized, altered, amplified, and so on even though the general themes were laid down by the leader.

Visions of Greatness

Another general characteristic of Brazilian intellectuals is that they are nationalists, and their nationalism consists of two volatile elements. First, there is love of country and second, there is hatred, or, at least, a suspicion of the foreigner.

Love of country is a mixture of three elements: celebration of the past, pride in the present, and the hope for a glorious future. A mature nationalism stresses love of country over hatred of the foreigner and depends upon present accomplishments instead of dwelling on the past or relying on an uncertain future. [13]

---

[11] *O Globo* (Rio de Janeiro), 31 May 1960. Quoted from José Honório Rodrigues, "La Política Internacional del Brasil y África," *FORO Internacional* (Mexico City), January-March 1964, p. 317. In the same speech, he added this thought on Brazilian leadership: "The great states that are born in Asia and Africa need to find in the international maturity of Brazil the spirit they lack for this inevitable emancipation so that it may be accomplished in the shortest time possible."

[12] A similar, but smaller spate of books and articles came after Kubitschek announced his "Operação Pan-Americana." Nothing remotely resembling the OPA had been suggested earlier by any Brazilian writer.

[13] As an example, American nationalism in the nineteenth century depended a great deal on anti-British feeling, which in duration and intensity far outdid the anticommunism of the 1950s.

Thus, while Brazilian intellectuals are nationalists, the emphasis will vary from writer to writer.[14] Roberto Campos makes a useful distinction between nationalists by labelling them either pragmatic and functional or romantic and temperamental. The romantics, he argues, propose a developmental theory which advocates "more consumption, more investment, and less capital inflow." And further: "They want the national entrepreneur strengthened, but mutilate him with disturbing interventions by the state and incompetent manipulation of the price system. They want the results of development, but not the means to achieve it. Many of them, though they do not confess it, favor the dangerous surgery of revolution." [15]

The pragmatic nationalist, says Campos, tries to work within present institutions, and prefers reform over revolution. And on a personal note, he concludes:

As to myself, I shall continue considering myself a pragmatic nationalist. I renounce the temptation of mobilizing resentment in order to gain the authority to plan development. I would rather strengthen the national entrepreneur than merely antagonize the foreigner. I would want the state not to do what it cannot do, in order to do what it should do. I prefer to love my own country rather than to hate the others.[16]

But whether pragmatic or romantic, Brazilian intellectuals have been inspired by their country's vastness to work out lofty conceptions of Brazil's future role in world politics. In this they are all romantic.

It has always been so. In 1627, a native Brazilian and Franciscan friar, Vicente do Salvador, concluded his history of Brazil with a prediction of a great future for his country, after praising its wealth, size, and potential population. A century later, the second history of the colony, written by Sebastião da Rocha Pita, repeated and elaborated upon these themes, and concluded that Brazil alone was an "earthly paradise." At least a half-dozen other historians wrote in similar terms during the eighteenth century.[17]

---

[14] Brazil's intellectuals contrast sharply with the great majority of their American counterparts, which has been internationalist since the end of World War I.

[15] Roberto Campos, *Reflections on Latin American Development* (Austin: University of Texas Press, 1967), p. 57.

[16] Ibid., p. 57.

[17] E. Bradford Burns, *Nationalism in Brazil: A Historical Survey* (New York: Praeger, 1968), pp. 14 and 20-21. At the end of that century, Alexandre Rodrigues Ferreira explored the Amazon region and wrote *Diário da Viagem Filosófica*, which was the first work to emphasize the area's incalculable wealth. Ibid., p. 23.

In the following century these themes were steadily developed by the Instituto Histórico e Geográfico Brasileiro, whose journal expanded upon Brazil's magnificent resources and demonstrated distrust of foreigners, especially when they undertook to write Brazilian history. The culmination came with the appearance of Afonso Celso's work, *Porque Me Ufano do Meu País,* published in 1900 (with thirteen subsequent editions). Celso wrote of Brazil's magnificence (size, wealth, and beauty), and, in addition, reviewed its historical accomplishments.[18] While Brazilian intellectuals had laid the foundation for nationalism, they had not worked out specifically a role for Brazil in the world arena. And in the meantime, the actual foreign policy makers, especially after Rio-Branco, pursued a strategy that rested on national survival through a balance of power in South America and friendship with the United States for protection against extra-continental aggressors.

By the end of World War II, a few Brazilian intellectuals began questioning traditional doctrine and advocating a larger role for Brazil in world affairs. For example, in *Um Programa Política Exterior para o Brasil,* Renato Castelo Branco asserted that the war had destroyed the old realities of international life. Thus, in the Latin world, France was "reviled" for her defeat; Italy was "reduced to complete impotence"; and Spain, Portugal, and Argentina, with their fascist-style politics, were out of step with triumphant democracy. Thus, through a process of elimination, Brazil emerges as the Latin world's "most authoritative voice . . . heard in the peace conferences."[19]

Although Castelo Branco admitted that Brazil had not yet become a first-class power, he held that its resources and population made this nearly inevitable. With this in mind, Castelo Branco constructed a three-faceted foreign policy: First, through ties of race, culture, and religion, Brazil is linked to the Latin world. Brazil should lead this

---

[18] Ibid., pp. 39-41 and 54-55. Coupled with love of country, however, was a developing dislike for the foreigner. In the nineteenth century, Brazilians first were anti-Portuguese, then anti-British. In addition, there was anti-Spanish Americanism. The latter was rooted in the boundary wars with Argentina and a feeling of superiority. Brazil had remained strong and viable, while Spanish America had broken up into weak, turbulent, and quarreling states. However, Brazilian nationalism was never solely nor primarily dependent on xenophobia. The theme of Brazilian greatness was too strong and plausible for that to happen. Ibid., pp. 33-37.

[19] Renato Castelo Branco, *Um Programa Política Exterior para o Brasil* (São Paulo: Editôra Brasiliense Ltda., 1945). All quotes on p. 19. The author was an ethnographer and a poet.

bloc and also encourage immigration from Latin countries in order to counter Brazil's German and Japanese communities.[20]

Second, Brazil is part of the Anglo-Saxon world because of similar political institutions. It is also dependent on military and economic aid from the Anglo-Saxon nations. On the other hand, the latter, especially the North Americans, need Brazil for its raw materials, its bases, and its stabilizing effect on volatile South America. This double dependency would be the basis for a genuine partnership between the two great nations of the Western Hemisphere.[21]

Third, Brazil is linked to South America. (This was emphasized during World War II when traditional markets were disrupted, leading to development of new markets in Latin America.) Thus, when South American political unity becomes a serious matter, Brazil should exercise leadership.[22]

Castelo Branco had broken away from the old thinking, but he was an exception. Thirteen years passed before Brazil's traditional foreign policy was subjected to another critique, this time by Paulo Duarte, editor of *Anhembi,* an influential journal of politics in the 1950s. Duarte first criticized the idea that Brazil's role in world politics had to be limited since its closeness to the United States prevented any radical departures. He argued that a nation could only advance by breaking out of its "geographic milieu." In support of this contention he cited the push of the Greek city-state into Asia, the Romans and Arabs into the Mediterranean, and the Americans into the Pacific.

Others responded that this line of argument is irrelevant in the modern world: with today's technology, one *always* has a powerful neighbor. Duarte replied that Canada and Yugoslavia, much smaller and much closer to great powers than Brazil, maintain relatively independent and far-ranging foreign policies.[23]

It had also been argued that new approaches in Brazilian foreign policy would mean leaving the old alliance and "falling into the Muscovite embrace." Duarte denied this, and challenged his critics to explain how a new anti-colonialist posture could affect Brazil's "integral and sincere

---

[20] Ibid., pp. 33-36.

[21] Ibid., pp. 37-43.

[22] Ibid., p. 49.

[23] Paulo Duarte, "Política Exterior Independente," *Anhembi* (Rio de Janeiro), February 1958, pp. 517-518. Duarte was apparently the first to use the phrase "independent foreign policy."

military alliance with the United States in case of a direct conflict with Russia." [24]

Duarte challenged the traditional doctrine of national security through a regional balance of power and strategic protection from the U.S. by ignoring the first and accepting the latter only on the condition that Brazil retain its diplomatic freedom short of outright desertion to the enemy or neutralism. Moreover, he argued, there is besides national security one other basic principle: the securing of "highly moral objectives." [25] The latter was embodied in Brazil's proposed search for leadership over a bloc of countries, that is, the Afro-Asian bloc, who are, in Duarte's view, opposed to any type of oppression or intervention whether totalitarian or colonialist. [26] And he concluded: "We will preserve our military alliance with the United States but at the same time we will reinforce our security by the prestige that we will gain from the understandings we make not only with the Afro-Asian countries, but also with those countries of the free world which view current events with less reactionary eyes. . . ." [27]

Duarte had entered into unexplored territory, and no one would follow until Quadros began his campaign. [28] After that, intellectuals would shift their attention away from economic nationalism [29] and begin seriously thinking about their country's *Weltpolitik*. When that happened, however, policy makers were suddenly presented with a tempting variety of scenarios Brazil could follow, and we shall attempt to outline those that seem both plausible and likely to be adopted—at least in part.

We begin with the grandest: Brazil is destined to be a world power, perhaps *the* world power. This has been most clearly articulated by an army officer, General António de Souza Junior:

> No other country of the world equals it [Brazil] in possibilities. With a surface that is approximately half of South America, this vast territory introduces a nearly perfect geographic unity, a complete structural geophysical and political

24 Ibid., p. 520.

25 Ibid., p. 522.

26 Ibid.

27 Ibid.

28 Unfortunately for those who like neat patterns of historic causality, there is no evidence that Quadros read Duarte's article. A Brazilian foreign service officer stated to the author that *he* gave Jânio Quadros the idea when the latter visited Tokyo on his preinaugural world tour.

29 After all, it did give the impression that Brazil was just another banana republic struggling to win back its own bananas.

unity. In this immense country, there are not encountered any really inhospitable regions; there are no deserts or steppes, nor chains of high mountains. Its potential useful or productive area is 90% of its total area. . . . From the demographic point of view it is admitted that the Brazilian territory could shelter 900 million inhabitants or 1,200 million according to some estimates. . . . Mineral resources and energy potential of Brazil are immense and only now are beginning to be practically exploited. . . . without racial discrimination, without problems of alienated minorities, but on the contrary, united by the same language, by the same political-social system, by the same traditions, Brazil is . . . the greatest Potential Power that is emerging.[30]

Such a vision is not confined to the military mind. Best-selling author, Pimental Gomes, for one, even predicts the date of Brazil's superpower apotheosis: the year 2000. His prose bristles with objectives to be seized:

The position of Brazil in South America is *sui generis*. It is not repeated in any other country, in any other continent. . . . It has more usable land than all the other South American countries combined. It extends itself to . . . the Atlantic coast, the most important ocean. . . . The Pacific is easily accessible. São Pedro and São Paulo, Fernando de Noronha, Trinidade, Martim Vaz are lonely sentinels in the Atlantic, precious points of support in peace and war. We need Ascension, St. Helena, Tristão da Cunha, Gough, and Bouvet. Cape Verde could be a Brazilian state. It could have its advantages. Perhaps an honorable agreement might be possible with Portugal. And a slice of the Antarctic should come to us. . . . We ought to claim it immediately.[31]

And in case his readers missed the point, Gomes *extended* this strategy in his next book:

There are no friendships among nations. It was always so. John Foster Dulles said on one occasion . . . "The United States has no friends: it has interests." Also the Soviet Union, China, Great Britain, and France, the Germanies, Italy, only have interests. It should not be. But unfortunately it is. Brazil therefore has to act in the same way. International

[30] General António de Souza Junior, *O Brasil e a Terceira Guerra Mundial* (Rio de Janeiro: Biblioteca do Exército Editôra, 1959), pp. 269-270.
[31] Pimental Gomes, *O Brasil entre as Cinco Maiores Potências no Fim neste Século* (Rio de Janeiro: Editôra Leitura, 1964), pp. 15-16.

aid . . . is based on the interests of the countries that give it even though they seem absolutely disinterested. It would not be just for a people to pay taxes and to sacrifice themselves in order to make another people great. Only a madman would believe that. Unfortunately, in Brazil . . . there are some who still believe this.[32]

This relentless realpolitik ends with the recommendation that Brazil adopt a policy "entirely Brazilian," though commitments to the Western world should not be entirely forgotten.[33]

Brazil and the Third World

The geopoliticians are not alone in thinking big. Many Brazilian intellectuals have taken up where Quadros left off in designing a strategy that would give Brazil leadership over the recently sovereign, ex-colonial areas.

While the intelligentsia habitually refer to the "Afro-Asian bloc," they have had difficulty making an argument for close relations with Asia. Amilcar Alencastre finds a common suffering from low prices for tropical raw materials.[34] Adolpho Menezes, a diplomat with experience in Indonesia, mentions Brazil's Chinese and Japanese immigrants as possible links with Asia.[35] But on the whole this kind of argument reinforces the impression of Asian remoteness, rather than affinity.

Africa is another matter. That great continent has generated interest, indeed excitement, in men of widely varying political beliefs. At first that interest was rooted in national security. Even the left-wing journal, *Anhembi*, argued that "Brazil cannot help but be interested in the events that will be occurring in Africa in the next decades, since

---

[32] Pimental Gomes, *Porque não Somos uma Grande Potência* (Rio de Janeiro: Editôra Civilização Brasileira, 1965), p. 126.

[33] Ibid., p. 154. Gomes cites DeGaulle's France as an ideal model to emulate.

[34] Amilcar Alencastre, *Oswaldo Aranha: O Mundo Afro-Asiático e a Paz* (Rio de Janeiro: Capa de Fortunata, 1961), pp. 84-88. Alencastre suggests that Brazil has another toehold because of the spread of Portuguese culture to India (Goa), Ceylon, and Timor, and records the fact that 300 Portuguese words have become part of the Indonesian language. Alencastre devoted his next book exclusively to Africa. Amilcar Alencastre, *O Brasil, a África e o Futuro* (Rio de Janeiro: Editôra Laemmert: 1969).

[35] Adolpho Justo Bezerra de Menezes, *O Brasil e o Mundo Ásia-Africano*, 2d ed. (Rio de Janeiro: Irmãos Ponhetti, Editores, 1960), pp. 17-27.

a racist or Communist Africa would not be free of danger for the countries on the opposite side of the Atlantic." [36]

By 1960, however, interest in Africa—thanks in part to Quadros—went beyond Brazilian security. The conservative, Estanislaw Fishlowitz, for example, held that Brazil would influence African development because it had no colonial taint, and, unlike the United States, it had no military and political ties with the colonial powers—except for the "traditional sentimental friendship" with Portugal. He also contended that "racial democracy" and the large African contribution to Brazilian culture would help lay the basis for a Brazilian-African entente. [37]

Occasionally, history is used as another link with Africa. In particular, historian José Honório Rodrigues has developed this argument. For example, he states that Brazil and Africa enjoyed an intimate relationship that lasted for three centuries until the 1850s. Besides a flourishing commerce, Rodrigues recalls a heroic "Brazilian," Salvador Correia de Sa, who, in 1648, led an expedition from Rio de Janeiro to recapture Angola from the Dutch, who had "usurped" the colony seven years earlier. Brazilian trade with Angola immediately resumed, and the province became more dependent on Brazil than ever. [38] The image of Brazil as a liberator of an African state from European imperialism has certainly been appealing to Brazilian—if not to African—intellectuals.

Past contact and present compatibility, then, serve as the rationale for Brazil's role in Africa. What precisely that role *is*, however, becomes lost after one finishes the opening rationale. Usually those who speculate on such matters go on to criticize earlier policy or instruct Brazilian scholars to learn more about Africa. [39]

---

[36] Unsigned article, "Destino Político da Africa Negra," *Anhembi* (Rio de Janeiro), July 1955, p. 231. For a roughly similar but military opinion, see General Golbery do Couto e Silva, *Aspectos Geopolíticos do Brasil* (Rio de Janeiro: Biblioteca do Exército, 1957), pp. 27-28.

[37] Fishlowitz constructed the basic rationale that later writers would repeat. Unlike his more radical colleagues, however, Fishlowitz did not condemn colonialism out of hand. He argued that the colonial powers did set up a judicial order which defended personal and property rights and suppressed intertribal conflict and "the shameful slave trade and other abuses." E. Fishlowitz, "Subidos para a 'Doutrina Africana' do Brasil," *Revista Brasileira de Política Internacional,* March 1960, pp. 89 and 94.

[38] Rodrigues, *Brazil and Africa,* pp. 18-24.

[39] Ibid., p. 327, and Eduardo Portella, *Política Externa e Povo Livre* (São Paulo: Editôra Fulgor, 1963), pp. 20-21; Eduardo Portella, *África: Colonos e Cúmplices* (Rio de Janeiro: Editorial Prado Ltda., 1961), pp. 141-143.

On occasion it is suggested that Brazil must exercise leadership in the Third World, and that it is throwing away priceless opportunities for such leadership when it supports the United States or does not vote against Portugal in the U.N. General Assembly.[40] But the shape such leadership should take has never been defined. What exactly does it mean to lead? How should Brazil go about it? What would it cost Brazil? And what, specifically, would be the advantages? One could begin to fashion answers, but the point is that Brazilian intellectuals have not addressed themselves to these questions as yet.[41]

Perhaps because of the vastness and heterogeneity of the Third World, some Brazilian intellectuals have attempted to fashion policies that would involve only a part of that world. Two schemes are of special interest. The first may be called the Luso-Brazilian community; the second, the South Atlantic alliance.

Brazil as a South Atlantic Power

The first recognizes the immense problem of dealing with, much less leading, the Afro-Asian world. Instead, as Gilberto Freyre argues, Brazil can easily become the leader of the Portuguese-speaking world. He adds:

> This world may soon become a federation with a common citizenship and a number of other rights and responsibilities. . . . It is interesting to note the growing tendency of the new generations in Portuguese India, Portuguese Africa, in the Cape Verde Islands, and to a lesser extent the Azores, to follow inspirations and suggestions from Brazil.[42]

---

[40] Rodrigues, "La Política Internacional," pp. 322-324.

[41] Not all Brazilians share the general intellectual euphoria about Africa. Maria Leite Linhares, another historian, is skeptical of Brazilian success in any African diplomacy, and for three reasons: First, its much vaunted historical links with Africa are primarily based on the slave trade, about which Africans would rather forget and of which Brazilians should be ashamed. Second, Brazilian miscegenation is utterly meaningless to Africans, who, with few exceptions, do not live in racially pluralistic societies. And third, Africans are not about to break ties with Europe—especially economic ones—and opt for Brazilian leadership. Maria Y. Leite Linhares, "Brazilian Foreign Policy and Africa," *The World Today*, December 1962, pp. 532-540. In addition, Professor Artur Fereira Reis has pointed out the problem of trade competition in primary products. A. C. Fereira Reis, "África e Brasil: Relações e Competições," *Revista Brasileira de Política Internacional*, June 1963, pp. 209-222.

[42] Gilberto Freyre, *New World in the Tropics* (New York: Knopf, 1959), pp. 182-183.

Moreover, Freyre argues, even if Portugal were to change the status of Angola and Mozambique, "the people of Portuguese Africa look to ethnically democratic Brazil as their natural leader—not to some sub-Nehru. . . ." [43]

Despite the romanticism in much of Freyre's writing about the "Lusitanian character," [44] there is something immediate and practical about expanding relations with an area of Africa that has had long historical ties with Brazil.[45] Portugal too has solicited Brazil's support in preserving its presence in Africa with hints of trade preferences and shared responsibilities.

But even Portugal's friends see problems, most of them quite obvious. Overt Brazilian participation in such a community would not make relations with the rest of Africa any easier.[46] As long as Portugal is a *bête noire* of black Africa, no role short of an active, anti-Portuguese policy will do. But such an approach (which even Quadros and Goulart did not carry out) would have uncertain benefits and would at least until recently also have ended any hope of entry into Portuguese Africa.

In recent years, the official as well as the unofficial Brazilian imagination has been exercised regarding a South Atlantic alliance. The impetus, not surprisingly, has come from the military strategists, especially the navy's. For example, in a 1969 issue of *Segurança e Desenvolvimento,* Vice Admiral Acyr Dias de Carvalho Rocha speculated that in the event of a nuclear war, the Southern Hemisphere would probably survive intact. Thus, Argentina, Australia, South Africa, and Brazil—as leader—would have the task of reconstructing and, no doubt, dominating the world.[47]

---

[43] Gilberto Freyre, "Misconceptions of Brazil," *Foreign Affairs,* April 1962, pp. 460-461.

[44] See his *The Masters and the Slaves,* trans. Samuel Putnam, 2d rev. ed. (New York: Knopf, 1956), passim.

[45] Even the very unsentimental General Souza sees the possibilities of such a community, though it would pose problems for Brazil. Souza Junior, *O Brasil,* p. 141. Other Brazilian military men, although ambivalent about supporting Portugal openly, are very much afraid of pro-Communist guerrillas taking power in Angola, Mozambique, and Portuguese Guinea. Jon Rosenbaum, "Brazil's Foreign Policy: Developmentalism and Beyond," *Orbis,* Spring 1972, p. 78. Since the Portuguese coup, there has been a conspicuous silence about the guerrilla groups. Few Brazilian intellectuals, military or civilian, have supported Adolpho Menezes's suggestion to send non-white Brazilian soldiers to Portuguese Africa. Menezes, *O Brasil e o Mundo Ásia-Africano,* pp. 378-379.

[46] Souza Junior, *O Brasil,* pp. 139-145; Rodrigues, *Brazil and Africa,* p. 308; Portella, *África,* pp. 127-128.

[47] Brazil's trade with developed South Africa is greater than that with all the rest of sub-Saharan Africa.

At first glance, any cooperation with South Africa might seem unlikely in view of the latter's racial policies. Nevertheless, *Segurança e Desenvolvimento* also published an essay by air force General Augusto Teixeira Coimbra who argued that apartheid was not only non-racist, but that South Africa itself was viable.[48] Shortly after that essay appeared, rumors were reported circulating in Rio to the effect that Brazil, South Africa, and Argentina were about to sign a treaty to defend the South Atlantic from Soviet penetration. The rumors were sparked by an "unofficial" visit of a high-ranking South African cabinet minister. The rumors, in fact, were so prevalent that the normally aloof Itamaraty issued an official denial of any such agreement.[49] However, speculation did not cease, and later was revived when South African Airways initiated flights between the two countries.[50]

Thus, a South Atlantic alliance, while tempting and plausible on geopolitical grounds, has not yet emerged. But it is an option that some Brazilians seem to take seriously, and its time may come, especially after Brazil completes its ambitious naval expansion.

Brazil in Latin America

Brazilian intellectuals, gazing out over the South Atlantic and beyond, rarely glance backward at their own continent. Leadership of South America has not interested them much.[51] Outside of President Kubitschek's entourage, there was little support for his "Operação Pan-Americana." Rodrigues even considered it a serious diversion from the major tasks of Brazilian diplomacy—expanded ties with Africa.[52] Even the "traditional" role of mediator between the United States and Latin America has been supported in print by only one recent writer.[53]

In addition, some have attacked the priority given to developing Latin American trade. For instance, Paulo Duarte pointed out that

---

[48] Rosenbaum, "Brazil's Foreign Policy," pp. 81-82.
[49] Ibid.
[50] Ibid.
[51] The single exception is Plínio de Moura, a former Quadros aide, who called for Brazilian leadership of South America, since the U.S. has proved incapable of doing so after the death of Franklin Roosevelt. Plínio Rolim de Moura, *O Líder da América Latina* (São Paulo: Editôra e Distribuidora Universal, 1960), pp. 7-8 and 117-118.
[52] Rodrigues, "La Política Internacional," pp. 314-315.
[53] Gilberto Freyre, *Uma Política Transnacional de Cultura para o Brasil de Hoje* (Rio de Janeiro: Edições da Revista Brasileira do Estudos Políticos, 1960), pp. 53-54.

Brazil's exports were competitive with those of the rest of the region. In addition, he noted, the size of the markets available in South America will never come close to those already existing in Japan and China, and as far as the comparison of distance is concerned, the Latin American transportation network is so bad that costs within Latin America nearly equal shipping costs to the Orient.[54]

The truth is that since Brazil secured its borders and achieved military superiority, intellectuals have not taken Spanish America seriously. Furthermore, there is little point in thinking about leadership of a South American bloc when the benefits for Brazil as well as its neighbors are limited at best.[55]

United States-Brazilian Relations

South America is no longer the primary arena for Brazilian diplomacy, while the underdeveloped world—especially Africa—and the Communist countries have gotten increasing amounts of attention. But if the traditional focus on South America has altered, what now is the character of thought concerning Brazilian-American relations?

There is no other topic that is more controversial among Brazilian intellectuals, and nowhere is the division between "pragmatic" and "romantic" nationalists more clearly drawn. In the case of Africa, the romantics favor a large Afro-Asian policy, while the pragmatists tend to settle for the more manageable Luso-Brazilian community. But the issue of nationalism—love of country, hatred of the foreigner—is at the heart of any discussion of Brazil's relations with America.

First, one finds few intellectuals advocating the traditional relationship even among the pragmatists. Some like Mario Guimarães are still willing to give the United States credit for protecting the hemisphere,

---

[54] Paulo Duarto, "Política Externa Independente," *Anhembi* (Rio de Janeiro), February 1958, pp. 517-522.

[55] There is, of course, a certain amount of nervousness in Spanish America about alleged Brazilian designs on Bolivia and Paraguay. (One American observer has outlined scenarios that entail Brazilian intervention in Guyana and Uruguay.) However, despite the intervention rumors that circulated at the time of the 1970 Tupamaro kidnapping of a Brazilian diplomat, and some offhand remarks of a few military officers, there is little hard evidence that expansionism is taken seriously in Brazil. In the meantime, only one intellectual has written on this subject at length. See P. H. da Rocha Correa, *Brasil o as Guianas* (Catanduva, São Paulo: Irmãos Boso Editores e Livreiros, 1965), and *Rumos do Brasil* (Catanduva, São Paulo: Irmãos Boso Editores e Livreiros, 1965). See also Rosenbaum, "Brazil's Foreign Policy," pp. 75-79.

and Carlos Lacerda (at least until 1965) once proposed unreserved adherence to the American alliance:

> It is necessary to say clearly that at the moment there is only one hope for peace on earth; it is that Russia does not become stronger than the United States and that the balance of forces may be favorable to those who desire peace . . . because they love life and their creator.
> Any attempt to make Brazil neutral would not only weaken world peace, it would give an advantage to the totalitarian governments in their war against the freedom loving nations. . . . To neutralize Brazil is to weaken the alliance and the resistance of America.[56]

Most Brazilian intellectuals, including the pragmatists, have criticized the old policy and also have suggested new ways of handling the United States. Among the pragmatists, however, the criticism is limited, and it usually focuses on the need for the United States to accept Brazil as a serious power on its own. Henrique Valle, for example, has written that the U.S. must accept a new Brazilian policy which will seek to lead the Latin American bloc instead of acting as an interpreter and mediator—the old roles designed by Rio-Branco.[57]

Adolpho Menezes also argues for a selective alliance with the United States. He states that Brazil should follow America in its struggle with the Soviet Union, but that it should not defer to the United States on matters of African policy.[58]

Since selective disagreement seems to be the watchword of the pragmatists, they must reject neutralism. When neutralism was at its height of popularity in Brazil, the formidable Roberto Campos reviewed its possibilities. He admitted that a policy of nonalignment has one attractive advantage: concessions can be extracted from both sides and trade can be diversified.[59]

Nevertheless, Campos found that those arguing for neutrality had failed to think out their position. In the first place, they had not con-

---

[56] Mario Guimarães, *Política Exterior do Brasil: Atitude Conservadora e Não Inerte* (San Jose, Costa Rica: n.p., 1956), pp. 32-33; Carlos Lacerda, *O Poder das Ideias* (Rio de Janeiro: Distribuidora Record, 1963), p. 141.

[57] Valle held the second spot in the foreign ministry during Kubitschek's presidency. Henrique Valle, "Algums Aspectos das Relações Brasil-Estados Unidos," *Revista Brasileira de Política Internacional,* December 1961, p. 11.

[58] Adolpho Menezes, *O Brasil e o Mundo Ásia-Africano,* p. 329.

[59] Later, as planning minister, Roberto Campos signed a $100 million credit arrangement with the Soviet Union to finance hydroelectric projects.

sidered whether there is a "sufficient, cultural, philosophical or religious tradition . . . which may impede the disfiguration of the national character of the neutralist nation." [60] India and Egypt, he believed, possess a buffering religious tradition, but Brazil with its "superficial" Christianity does not.

Campos further argued that the neutralists had not considered the geopolitical problem that nonalignment presents. To be neutral requires sufficient distance from the centers of power, a condition Brazil fulfills. However, there is another requirement Brazil cannot meet: it is not the acknowledged leader of its region. Unlike India and Egypt, Brazil does not hold cultural sway over its neighbors. On balance, said Campos, his country could not carry out a successful policy of neutralism.

Campos concluded, however, that rejecting full-fledged neutralism did not rule out "tactical neutralism" or "selective alignment." He held that such approaches would not involve a mathematically precise middle position between the blocs, but would change from issue to issue depending on the benefits that might be accrued to satisfy Brazil's overriding national interest: economic development.[61]

Left-wing critics have suggested that Brazil has sought a "privileged satellite" status with the United States. This means that in return for generous economic assistance, Brazil would act as "chief agent" in South America for its North American benefactor. As agent, it would presumably police the area, preventing any obnoxiously radical regime from taking power. This particular option, however, has not received any support from civilian intellectuals, even the pragmatic nationalists.[62]

Romantic Nationalism and the United States

But while the pragmatists argued for a selective revision in relations, the romantic nationalists demanded fundamental change. For Roque

---

[60] Roberto Campos, "Sobre Conceito de Neutralismo," *Revista Brasileira de Política Internacional,* September 1961, p. 6.

[61] Ibid., pp. 6-8. See also Campos's speech that was delivered to the Pan-American Society on 19 December 1962 and reprinted in *Brazilian Bulletin,* no. 424 (January 1963).

[62] The satellite scenario was suggested by an Argentine journalist, Rogelio Garcia Lupo, in a Uruguayan newspaper, *Marcha.* In the article he charged that General Golbery Couto e Silva, chief of Brazilian military intelligence, had argued in a position paper that "the United States will put all of South America under the tutelage of Brazil, in the same way that Great Britain handed domination of the hemisphere over to the United States in the nineteenth century." Reprinted in *Atlas,* November 1965, p. 286.

Gadelha de Melo, the cold war is a ploy on the part of the U.S. to squeeze out economic advantages from the underdeveloped world. Worse, in case of real war, the United States would attempt to get Latin America, especially Brazil, to join the conflict. And that could mean the latter's nuclear annihilation.[63]

Others do not need such a threat to support their demands for independence from America. Limeira Tejo argued in 1966 (that is, *after* the military takeover) that collaboration with the U.S. would inevitably lead to satellization. The reason, he claimed, is simple: the U.S. has an increasing need for raw materials. It has been barred from Asia and Africa—leaving only Brazil as a major supplier.[64]

Since the present relationship is so unsatisfactory, what do the romantics wish to replace it with? This is not very clear. Aligning with the nonaligned is never seriously suggested, nor is allying with any of the Communist nations. It is almost as if the romantics believe that once Brazil has declared its independence, its status as a great power will be automatically achieved. There would be no need for alignment with anyone.

Further, no one seems willing to spell out the consequences of a new American policy. After all, the U.S. remains the principal market for Brazilian exports.

The Intellectuals and Economic Development

Political relations between Brazil and the United States, while controversial, have not generated the heat that economic relations have. Since Vargas's 1950 presidential campaign, and especially after his suicide, the lines of battle have been sharply drawn between two camps, and the focus has been private investment.

Most of the discussion is on an emotional level and is not founded on an economic analysis of gains and losses. This is particularly true of the romantics, among whom is J. Salgado Freire:

> The majority of companies that today exploit us are North American. . . . The astronomical profits that leave the country, drawn from all our effort, impoverish us, make us paupers,

---

[63] Roque Gadelha de Melo, "Neutralidade do Brasil: Imperativo Constitucional," *Revista Brasiliense* (Rio de Janeiro), March-April 1959, pp. 174-175.

[64] Limeira Tejo, "Brasil, País Satelite?" *Cadernos Brasileiros* (Rio de Janeiro), July-August 1966, p. 28.

46

debilitate us, and aggravate our misery considerably. The capitalists rob us, but they tell us that they are helping us; they make scandalous investments . . . with highly impertinent airs of philanthropy.[65]

Less impassioned discussions are difficult to find among Brazilian intellectuals, where love of country and xenophobia are so inextricably mixed. Only a few journals regularly publish technically sound articles.[66]

Probably the most controversial aspect of foreign investment is the question of profit remittances. On this issue there are only two opinions—and precious little shading between them.

The romantics have made this their central issue. Maia Neto, who is representative, believes profit remittances to be merely colonial exploitation in a new form. The Portuguese had exploited Brazil openly by reserving exclusive trade privileges for themselves. Today, he charges, modern colonialists use more subtle, but equally effective, means of exploitation. They move in with glib promises of progress, but proceed to help themselves to Brazil's riches.[67] Salgado Freire supports this oft-made point by citing data which ostensibly show that foreign companies take profits out of the country that are many times their original investment.[68]

But it does not matter much what data are used (or how they are obtained); for the romantics, the answer is nearly always the same: foreign investors are suction pumps (*bombas da sucção*) siphoning off the incredible wealth of Brazil. And the pumps will keep working until a new profit-remittance law is passed.

Pragmatic nationalists have challenged this thesis. Among them, Roberto Campos has been the most prominent. He has observed that in Latin America generally, there has always been a search for panaceas to explain and to overcome the region's backwardness. Industrialization, agrarian reform, and stabilization of export-product prices have all been invoked in the past. In Brazil, according to Campos, the chief

---

[65] J. Salgado Freire, *Para Onde Vai o Brasil? Grandezas e Misérias do Nosso Desenvolvimento* (Rio de Janeiro: Conquista, 1959), pp. 208-209 and 212-213.
[66] *Digesto Econômico* and *Conjuntura Econômica* are exceptions.
[67] Maia Neto, *Brasil: Guerra Quente na América Latina* (Rio de Janeiro: Editôra Civilização Brasileira, 1965), pp. 40-41.
[68] J. Salgado Freire, *Para Onde Vai o Brasil,* p. 210. His data are highly suspect. In the table which shows original investment and total profits earned, no time period is indicated, no adjustment for inflation is made, nor is an explanation given on how or where the statistics were obtained or how much of the total profits were actually remitted.

problem is profit remittances. End this, the romantics cry, and Brazilian poverty will end:

> Even in the presidential campaign [of 1960], the problem was mixed up with the fundamental questions. . . . No one meanwhile seems to have given himself the task of finding out if the problem exists. Perhaps because it smacks of an ideological question if the facts are contrary. So much the worse for the facts. . . . I am convinced that the only activity of the prosperous and organized research among us is the search for scapegoats.[69]

Campos has produced his own data on profit remittances. He found that annual profit remittances come to less than 0.5 percent of Brazil's gross domestic product. Therefore, remittances absorb less than 2 percent of the foreign exchange Brazil uses annually. If royalties are included, the figure goes up to 2.6 percent. If interest on loans is added, the total goes to 6 percent. Stopping remittances, then, would hardly stem Brazil's foreign-exchange drain. Meanwhile, restrictions on profit remittances might discourage new investment, damaging the balance of payments rather than improving it.[70]

Campos has also cited other evidence in making his case for foreign investment. He has pointed out that if the romantic nationalists were correct, São Paulo, "exploited by an enormous concentration of foreign capital, ought to be poor; Piauí . . . ought to be rich." [71] (This point has never been answered by Campos's critics.) He has also reminded the romantics of the fact that in the nineteenth century Brazil received only small amounts of outside capital and grew slowly, while the United States welcomed foreign investment and developed rapidly.[72]

Campos, like most pragmatists, does not simply favor the status quo. He has advocated measures to "Brazilianize" foreign investment: Foreign firms should be compelled to sell shares to Brazilians. Such firms should be made to liquidate their debts before foreign exchange is

---

69 Roberto Campos, "Dove Si Grida Non e Vera Scienza . . ." *Correio da Manhã* (Rio de Janeiro), 4 December 1960, p. 2. Reprinted in his *A Moeda, O Govêrno e o Tempo* (Rio de Janeiro: APEC Editôra, 1964), pp. 59-60.

70 Ibid., pp. 59-61.

71 Roberto Campos, "A Imbecilidade dos 'Slogans,' " *Digesto Econômico,* January-February 1963, p. 21.

72 Ibid. For example, Eugenio Gudin, another pragmatist, has long advocated the ending of special privileges for the automobile industry, especially the favorable exchange rates extended to imports needed by the industry. Eugenio Gudin, *Analise de Problemas Brasileiros, 1958-1964* (Rio de Janeiro: Livraria Agir Editôra,1965), pp. 330-331.

granted. Income tax rates of foreign residents should be adjusted upward. Antitrust legislation should be passed against foreign and national monopolies to ensure competition without punishing enterprise. But, he adds, "Trusts are spoken of a lot; they are discerned where they do not exist; there is attributed to them quite often an absolutely super-human power." [73]

The foreign-investment debate has been marked by personal abuse. The romantics, especially, have resorted to the *ad hominem* technique. At times the charges are a bit vague. Dagoberto Salles, for example, has asserted that Brazilian defenders of American investment are launching "dense fogs of false economic science and adventurous programmatic declarations . . . so that in the uproar, policies favorable to foreign interests would be adopted." [74] At other times, the charge is quite specific. Those who favor American investment on any terms are *entreguistas*—traitors who give away the national patrimony to foreigners.[75] Occasionally the polemic turns to pure personal abuse. One ultra-nationalist turned on Roberto Campos: "So when in Brazil Roberto Campos (Bob Fields) proposes the ending of Petrobrás and the concession on the part of sedimentary areas to national and foreign companies, he does not speak for himself: he hands on a message from the State Department, he transmits orders from Ellis O. Briggs." [76]

Those under attack have not remained silent, however. One critic of romantic nationalism, Gustavo Corção, has accused one of his opponents of writing a book filled with "gross insults and evangelical citations," and giving evidence of a "mental retardation, a shrinking

---

[73] Campos, *A Moeda*, pp. 64-66. Compare Moacyr Ribeiro who wrote: ". . . a capitalist monopoly is an affront to the dignity and to the sovereignty of the weak countries. We are seeing a whole continent in a state of poverty through the force of the capitalist concentration of the United States. Why? Because capitalism exercises a force of attraction identical to that of universal gravitation. It is so fabulous, this 'X' force, that we have to take an opposite tack with velocity equal to 'X' in order to escape its attraction." Moacyr Ribeiro, *Jânio Deposto* (Rio de Janeiro: n.p., 1962), p. 150. To this Campos has replied: "I imagine that if an atomic bomb destroyed the North American suction pump, we would not become richer. Our leftists would have to find a new slogan to explain our underdevelopment." Campos, "A Imbecilidade," p. 21.

[74] Dagoberto Salles, *As Razões do Nacionalismo* (São Paulo: Editôra Fulgor, 1959), p. 165.

[75] Alberto Guerreiro Ramos, *O Problema Nacional do Brasil* (Rio de Janeiro: Editôra Saga, 1960), pp. 252-253.

[76] Gondim de Fonseca, "Os Antinacionalistas e a Próxima Ditura," in Adalgisa Nery, ed., *Sopram Os Ventos da Liberdade* (São Paulo: Editôra Fulgor, 1959), pp. 100-101.

of the faculties, a simplification of reasoning that surpasses everything one can imagine." [77] And Roberto Campos, in reply to a question on *entreguismo*, countered: "Many people see in the epithet *entreguista*, with which we insult some of our greatest patriots and finest technicians, an example of bad faith. It is not even that. It is an example of simple stupidity." [78]

Nationalism and Economic Success

The debate that has now raged for twenty years will go on, and it will continue to have its effect on U.S.-Brazilian relations. It would be a serious mistake to assume that the military takeover of 1964 has ended the issue in favor of the pragmatists. Even while record rates of foreign investment pour into the country, the left, despite losses and censorship, continues to campaign, with no interference from the regime as long as the criticism is confined to foreigners. In view of these restrictions, anti-American sentiment could be even more virulent in the future. [79]

The romantic nationalists have had their effect in the past. Remittance restrictions were imposed during the Vargas years and again in 1962, and in recent years new restrictions have been placed on foreign investment. [80] Moreover, the nationalists have made certain institutions and policies nearly untouchable, especially Petrobrás and the public utilities.

But romantic nationalists, despite their influence, are not as powerful in Brazil as they are in the rest of the world. This is because their master premise entails Brazil's gross inferiority relative to the U.S. Such notions of weakness run against the strong general belief in Brazilian greatness—a greatness that consists of more than mere potential.

Furthermore, Brazil's recent economic spurt has presented the left-wing nationalists with a problem: success has been achieved without

---

[77] Gustavo Corção, "Nacionalismo," *Digesto Econômico*, November-December 1958, p. 92.

[78] Roberto Campos, "The United States and Brazil: A Diplomatic View," in Irving Louis Horowitz, ed., *Revolution in Brazil* (New York: Dutton, 1964), pp. 360-361.

[79] For example, in his recent history of Brazilian-American relations, Moniz Bandeira argues at great length on the imperialist designs of the U.S. Moniz Bandeira, *Presença dos Estados Unidos no Brasil* (Rio de Janeiro: Civilização Brasileira, 1973).

[80] Some limitations have been placed on mineral extraction and investment in the Amazon. The new Geisel government, of course, is free to alter these restrictions.

following their autarkic prescription. Indeed, foreign investment has played a major role in Brazil's revival.

One method of dealing with this issue is to ignore it. Instead of focusing on Brazil, some of the nationalist writers extend their analysis to all of Latin America. The new literature on dependency to which Brazilians have contributed attempts, for example, to explain Latin American stagnation in general. Within this school of thought, there is widespread agreement on the nature of the problem, although there are marked differences when it comes to solutions. Hélio Jaguaribe, a Brazilian sociologist, has probably contributed most to the dependency literature,[81] and his central argument begins with the observation that underdevelopment is "the most general and salient of Latin America's structural characteristics." [82] A prime feature associated with under-development is economic stagnation, that is to say, underdevelopment is not (even gradually) being eliminated. Jaguaribe argues that stagnation, in fact, has characterized the region for the last two decades largely as a result of insufficient domestic effective demand. This, in turn, is because of another feature of Latin American societies, marginality: a majority of people are not participating either as producers or consumers.[83]

According to Jaguaribe, economic stagnation has left Latin America's ruling elites with a problem. If they chose to end marginality, and thus increase domestic demand, they would also create new political forces that could remove them from power. Therefore, they have chosen (or permitted to happen) denationalization as the way out. If they cannot save themselves, the foreigner will do it for them. Consequently, the economy is penetrated by foreign investors with the most important sectors (mining and manufacturing) soon controlled by outsiders. Cultural denationalization occurs simultaneously, especially in science and technology, with Latin America becoming dependent on foreign knowledge which is not even adapted to local conditions.[84]

---

[81] The latest and fullest treatment of Hélio Jaguaribe's analysis can be found in his *Political Development: A General Theory and a Latin American Case Study* (New York: Harper and Row, 1973). A more condensed version of his views is found in *La Dependéncia Politíca-Económica de América Latina* (Mexico City: Siglo Vientíuno Editores, 1970), pp. 1-85.

[82] Jaguaribe, *Political Development,* p. 403.

[83] Ibid., pp. 404-410.

[84] Ibid., 417-418.

Finally, argues Jaguaribe, Latin America is experiencing politico-military denationalization. This is a two-part process: First, the military, despite its nationalistic self-image, gets its weapons, often its training, and its doctrines (including attitudes toward communism) from the United States. When the military seizes power from the civilians, then the political system as a whole becomes denationalized since the new ruling elite, the armed forces, has become so dependent on foreigners.[85]

Denationalization eventually results in a dependency relationship between Latin America and the United States. The ruling elites of Latin America (much less the masses) are no longer in control of their own countries' affairs. They cannot execute the economic and political policies (which Washington would never approve) needed to break out of the stagnation trap.

Jaguaribe's prescription is not as neatly precise as his pathological analysis. First (and unlike many of his colleagues) he has expressed skepticism about revolution, especially the models that are discussed most in Latin America, that is, the Cuban and the Chinese. He does hold out hope for reformist regimes succeeding, though they have less than two decades to overcome stagnation. (By the 1990s at the latest, according to Jaguaribe, most of Latin America will experience societal explosions unless changes are made.) In Jaguaribe's estimation, the type of reformist regime most relevant is, oddly enough, the nationalist military. Peru, Colombia, Argentina, Ecuador, and Brazil qualify for this model.[86] But time is running out, and reformist regimes have a high rate of failure even under the best of circumstances. Other dependency theorists are even skimpier in their prescriptions although most have a predilection for revolution.

The dependency school borrows heavily from Marxism, especially in its prime assumption that capitalism is the driving force behind the creation of dependency relationships in Latin America. Teutónio dos Santos, for example, quarrels only with Lenin on one point in his analysis of imperialism. According to dos Santos, Lenin, unfortunately, was too concerned with the conditions within the capitalist countries which drove them to imperialist adventures. At the same time, he paid little attention to the conditions within the underdeveloped world that permitted, even encouraged, the spread of imperialism.[87]

---

[85] Ibid., pp. 418-425.
[86] Ibid.
[87] Teutónio dos Santos, "Crisis de la Teoria del Desarollo," in Jaguaribe, ed., La Dependéncia, pp. 175-176.

52

Despite its debt to Marxism (and a certain smugness about the "scientific" nature of its investigation), dependency theory offers a broader outlook and a more sweeping analysis than that of most romantic nationalists. The major weakness of the dependency writers is that they seldom deal with Brazil specifically. But it is clear that some of their concerns—for example, cultural denationalization—have been picked up by recent Brazilian regimes. And if Brazil's economic drive were to falter, then the ready-made explanations of failure provided by Jaguaribe and the others might appear highly persuasive, setting off a chain reaction resulting in weakened ties with the United States and the other developed nations.

What is the future course of nationalism in Brazil and how will it affect the United States? The answers are not clear, and in this lies the United States's hope. Among the Spanish-American nations there is only a small chance that nationalism will become less xenophobic. Brazil, on the other hand, may well advance beyond mere anti-Americanism. It is true that in the past Brazilian nationalism has depended on anti-foreign feeling, and that sentiment's strength has been directly proportional to Brazil's dependence on foreigners—Portuguese, British, and Americans. Lessening that dependence (which U.S. policy makers have done in the last five years) is a necessary though not sufficient step toward maintaining good relations with Brazil.

In the meantime, full Brazilian development is decades away, and the intellectuals are still badly torn with regard to the United States. For the last two decades, the intelligentsia has sought a new role for Brazil: the old policy lines worked out by Rio-Branco are now considered insufficient or rejected entirely by most writers. At the same time, Brazilian policy makers, after a number of false starts, have proven eclectic in taking ideas from the intelligentsia, although only a few intellectuals have even begun to think systematically about foreign policy.

For centuries, there never has been any question of Brazilian greatness among the "scribblers." But the very self-evidence of this greatness to them has prevented careful thinking about a strategy that would best exploit Brazil's opportunities. In short, what the nation's greatness implies for Brazil in the world arena has yet to be worked out.

4

The Policy Makers:
Itamaraty and the Military

As much as intellectuals have helped draw up Brazil's future options, and as much as they would like to influence policy directly, they still remain at the periphery of actual decision making. In that, they are not too different from their American counterparts.

In the United States, however, the policy-making process is far more complex than in Brazil, and it involves a host of actors, some of whom know their lines, while others do not. The President and his immediate advisors, of course, are critical. Indeed, it is all but unthinkable to Americans that foreign policy could be the private preserve of anyone but the President. Besides the chief executive, other agencies responsible for national security, such as the Department of Defense and the Central Intelligence Agency, also play a large role. The traditional foreign affairs bureaucracy, the Department of State, remains important, although most observers never tire of writing about its decline. The Treasury Department as well as other agencies participate in the foreign-policy process. Even the U.S. Congress seems to be taking its first, faltering steps back to genuine influence over the conduct of American foreign affairs.

In Brazil, the process is a good deal simpler. Only two institutions are vitally important in shaping foreign policy: the foreign ministry, Itamaraty, and the military. The Brazilian president, congress, and the other ministries play marginal roles, and this is unlikely to change in the next decade.

If senior foreign service and military officers are predominant, what precisely is the role of each in foreign policy? What are their views now, and what, if any, changes in outlook will come in the future?

In cases of differences between the foreign ministry and the armed forces, who prevails? Will both continue to dominate foreign policy or will others share in the process, and above all, what will be the effect of all this on relations with the United States?

Itamaraty and the World

Itamaraty continues to be very much the center of policy making, and, by all appearances, it intends to remain so. On this point, its friends and critics, foreign and domestic, all agree. And they have little choice. Itamaraty traditionally has taken the major responsibility, often with little or no executive control, for creating Brazil's foreign policy.[1]

Historically, Itamaraty has been in the middle of the process since the empire, when foreign ministers and their small staffs carried out the external business of Brazil without much direction or interference from the emperor—even in times of crisis.[2] In the early, formative period of the republic, Baron Rio-Branco remained foreign minister under four presidents and performed so capably that he had little need or desire for supervision.[3] Moreover, Rio-Branco insured the perpetuation of the ministry's influence by reorganizing it and selecting his subordinates and eventual successors. Thus, from the empire through the days of Rio-Branco to today's diplomats, Itamaraty has radiated an aura of complete competence and control in handling foreign affairs. It has also given the impression that outside influence is not welcome or even proper.

Itamaraty still performs the traditional tasks of diplomacy pretty much unassisted: The ministry negotiates with other countries on matters involving treaties. It gathers intelligence for policy makers. It represents Brazil in the international community, and it engages in consular activities.[4]

---

[1] José Honório Rodrigues, *Interêsse Nacional e Política Externa* (Rio de Janeiro: Civilização Brasileira, 1966), pp. 40-42.

[2] See C. F. Haring, *Empire in Brazil* (New York: W. W. Norton, 1968), for his account of the so-called "Christie Affair," which led to a break in diplomatic relations with Great Britain, but in which the foreign minister played the key role, not the emperor. See pp. 92-93.

[3] See above, pp. 17-19.

[4] Lincoln Gordon, "The Development of the United States Representation Overseas," pp. 11-12, in *The Representation of the United States Abroad* (New York: Columbia University Press, 1950), pp. 74-75.

Itamaraty and Negotiation. While the foreign minister (who is often a political figure) and the chief of state may oversee the writing of the major documents, the bread-and-butter agreements are worked out from beginning to end by the professional diplomatic corps. For example, the first trade mission sent to the Soviet Union (in November 1959) was led by Edmundo Barbosa da Silva, chief of Itamaraty's economics division. The role of the professional diplomat in East-West trade was further strengthened in 1960 through the creation of a so-called Mixed Executive Committee with headquarters in Rio and Moscow. The committee was composed of professionals and was set up to implement the trade agreement negotiated the previous year.[5] A similar procedure was used in drawing up a trade accord with Poland in 1963.[6]

The Intelligence Task. The second task of traditional diplomacy is that of intelligence gathering. The scope of this activity has increased enormously in the last half-century. Despite the new demand for information, which only a few of the world's foreign offices could fulfill, it is significant that Itamaraty has kept this mission within its control. Outside experts are not used, as historian José Honório Rodrigues has complained; the task is left exclusively to the professional insider.[7]

Once the raw data has been sent to Brasilia, study groups within Itamaraty analyze it. Occasionally findings of such study groups can be the focal point of controversy. For example, in January 1959 a foreign ministry study report, which flatly contradicted the recommendations of the National Development Bank of Brazil (BNDE) on Brazilian oil exploitation in Bolivia, was sent to President Kubitschek. The bank had recommended the use of American technical assistance because Brazil lacked the resources to fulfill its contract with Bolivia. The foreign ministry instead chose a "nationalist solution," which meant that foreign capital and technicians were rejected and the contract renegotiated. Itamaraty prevailed on this issue with the assistance of the congress.[8]

---

[5] See *Revista Brasileira de Política Internacional,* March 1960, pp. 166-168.

[6] *Revista Brasileira de Política Internacional,* March 1963, pp. 123-127. The principal negotiator for Brazil was Alúsio Regis Bittencourt, the assistant secretary-general for East Europe and Asian affairs.

[7] Rodrigues, *Interêsse Nacional,* p. 41.

[8] *Jornal do Brasil* (Rio de Janeiro), 15 January 1959, p. 9, and 18 January 1959, p. 4.

Itamaraty's Diplomacy. The third traditional duty of professional diplomats is to represent their country. This involves everything from the very routine matter of presenting credentials to the working out of a tense bilateral crisis.

One form of representation that has increased enormously in the last quarter-century is that of dealing with international organizations. Brazil is deeply involved in the United Nations.

Itamaraty and Exports. The final traditional duty concerns consular affairs. This involves far more than approving passports and stamping visas. Trade promotion is the new concern in Brazil, and it may be said that the country's recent boom is fueled by rapidly increasing exports. The latter became priority policy under President Costa e Silva, and not surprisingly, he assigned Itamaraty the twin tasks of trade expansion and technology acquisition.[9]. The ministry attempts to get better prices for Brazilian exports through negotiating international commodity agreements. It has sought better routes for Brazilian airlines. It has pushed Latin American trade liberalization vigorously, and it has defended Brazilian businessmen from the dumping practices of other countries. Finally, through the local research of its embassies, Itamaraty has attempted to find new markets for Brazilian goods.[10]

Indirectly, Itamaraty has established relations with at least one country for no other reason than that of watching a trade competitor. Of all the East African countries, only Kenya was chosen to have an embassy. In polite diplomatic language the embassy was to continue discussions on the problem of coffee. In addition, it was to keep an eye on the Kenyans and, if necessary, apply pressure before coffee conferences began.[11]

The Managing of Foreign Policy. How has Itamaraty managed to maintain control of the main lines of foreign policy while other foreign offices have increasingly surrendered theirs to others? [12] Itamaraty is an

---

9 *Boletim Especial* (Washington), 16 June 1967, p. 1.

10 *Jornal do Brasil* (Rio de Janeiro), 5 May 1966, p. 11.

11 *Boletim Especial* (Washington), 5 July 1967, p. 1.

12 For example, Massimo Bonanni, an Italian political scientist, has found the foreign offices of Western Europe challenged in policy making by the special expertise of the ministries of defense and treasury, agriculture, foreign trade and industry, and interior. What has happened is "each individual act comes up to involve the whole political sphere, the whole administration and every individual,

aloof institution. It attempts to convey the image of a group of professionals intent on their work—work that no one outside the ministry could possibly do better. And it operates in great secrecy. What internal disagreements exist are not often leaked. This is in marked contrast to the Brazilian military, whose differences of opinion regularly become the gossip of at least civilian elites, and what is leaked is quite specific, accurate, and complete.[13]

Aloofness not only gives the ministry as a whole great power, it also allows bureau chiefs within Itamaraty to wield great influence on their own. For example, in 1959, when Juscelino Kubitschek was pushing his policy of resuming trade and diplomatic relations with the Soviet Union, the chief of Itamaraty's political department, Odete de Carvalho e Souza, let it be known that she saw "no new element" in the issue and therefore was firmly opposed to Kubitschek's initiative. The latter, faced with a divided military, relented on diplomatic relations.[14]

The best known and most acrimonious dispute between Itamaraty and a Brazilian president involved Jânio Quadros and the then secretary-general, Vasco Leitão da Cunha. It began with a trade mission to Europe, whose chief, João Dantas, was personally selected by Quadros. Dantas, a newspaper publisher and early supporter of the president, proved industrious. In East Germany he signed a trade protocol within days of his arrival.[15] His action provoked an instant reaction among West German officials in Bonn, and since Brazil was negotiating the rescheduling of its debt to West Germany, the matter became embarrassing.[16]

Placed in this diplomatic difficulty, the secretary-general, apparently without consulting the foreign minister, released a note stating Dantas's

---

thereby enormously increasing the number of participants in the international political game and creating profound innovations in the traditional decisional structure." And he concludes: "The Ministry of Foreign Affairs is increasingly becoming just the spokesman for decisions which have been made elsewhere and sometimes other Ministries even represent it on the international scene. The functions of this Ministry are still an open question." Massimo Bonanni, "New International Policy Makers," *Le Spettatore Internazionale* (English edition), May-June 1967, pp. 185 and 209.

[13] See below, footnote 131, pp. 89-90.

[14] *Jornal do Brasil* (Rio de Janeiro), 2 August 1959, p. 4; and 21 August 1959, p. 4. Also *Última Hora* (Rio de Janeiro), 12 March 1959, p. 3. The foreign minister, Horácio Lafer, who had just been appointed, remained discreet and apparently was unable to exercise any influence over Senhora de Carvalho.

[15] *Hispanic American Report*, August 1961, p. 559.

[16] Ibid. The negotiating team was led by Roberto Campos. *Jornal do Brasil* (Rio de Janeiro), 31 May 1961, p. 4.

protocol was not binding since he was traveling "in a strictly private and personal manner without having any power to sign any document in the name of the Brazilian government." [17] The following day, Leitão da Cunha repeated his statement to the press, and took full responsibility for his action. In the meantime, much consternation was expressed in the Chamber of Deputies. One deputy demanded to know whether Dantas was empowered to sign the protocol or not, and if not, who was guilty of this "grave irregularity" which "leaves our Nation in a ridiculous position. . . ." [18]

Meanwhile, Quadros was doubly alarmed. On the one hand, Dantas had signed a document, which Quadros had specifically ordered him not to do. But on the other hand, he was a personal representative, and to disown him as the Itamaraty note implied would have been humiliating. Quadros's solution was to order the dismissal of Leitão da Cunha and send new instructions to Dantas. [19]

At this point, Leitão da Cunha's nominal superior, Foreign Minister Afonso Arinos, intervened and asked Quadros to reinstate the secretary-general. But Quadros still regarded Leitão da Cunha's act as insubordination and concluded he would make foreign policy "with or without Itamaraty." [20]

But the difficulty with West Germany could not be resolved by presidential bluster or even a shake-up at the foreign office. Two days after the interview, Afonso Arinos explained to the national Senate that no legally binding act had been signed by João Dantas, although the presidential representative was not acting in a mere private capacity as alleged by Leitão da Cunha. The document was a simple record of conversations, a joint communique about possible *future* understandings between two countries. [21] This artful, indeed inspired, compromise

---

17 *Jornal do Brasil* (Rio de Janeiro), 30 May 1961, p. 1; *Hispanic American Report,* August 1961, p. 559.

18 Quoted in *Jornal do Brasil* (Rio de Janeiro), 31 May 1961, p. 4.

19 In addition, Quadros let it be known that the now ex-secretary-general was guilty of "professional jealousy." *Jornal do Brasil* (Rio de Janeiro), 1 June 1961, p. 4. Meanwhile, the foreign minister, Afonso Arinos de Mello Franco, issued a statement to the press denying that Leitão da Cunha had been fired; he did admit that da Cunha was being considered for another position. See *Última Hora* (Rio de Janeiro), 3 June 1961, p. 4.

20 Quadros also hinted at the time that Leitão da Cunha's resistance was part of a foreign ministry plot to sabotage the new independent foreign policy. *Jornal do Brasil* (Rio de Janeiro), 4 June 1961, p. 3.

21 *Jornal do Brasil* (Rio de Janeiro), 7 June 1961, p. 4.

seemed to hold. (Later, the Dantas accord was repudiated, and matters smoothed over with Bonn.)

This incident is interesting in several respects: First, Itamaraty's highest officer did not hesitate to take on a personal representative of a highly aggressive chief executive. Second, although in this case it meant removal from office, the ministry protected its man to the extent that he was not dismissed from the service, and indeed would return in a few years as foreign minister, and later as ambassador to the United States. And finally, there were no subsequent instances of amateurs handling sensitive foreign matters without Itamaraty's explicit knowledge and approval.

Internal cohesion and a studied aloofness cannot entirely explain Itamaraty's defiance of presidential policy, much less its continued monopolizing of foreign policy. What then is its secret? There are, in fact, several secrets. First, Itamaraty has carefully built a reputation for hard work, efficiency, and integrity—virtues not very noticeable in the rest of the Brazilian bureaucracy—and it maintains its standards by admitting only those passing the most difficult examination given in the country. Admission to the foreign service on the basis of merit alone has been the law since 1946.[22]

Second, although the foreign office is a conservative institution, it has undergone periodic internal reform in order to strengthen its hold on foreign policy. Until 1960, the ministry had altered little in structure for over a century. Thus, in that year, when major foreign policy reforms were being put into effect, Itamaraty found itself having to carry out a new foreign policy with approximately the same organizational arrangements it had under the empire. It was organized along functional lines, and included political, economic, and administrative divisions. This left Itamaraty with a number of bureaucratic anomalies. For example, with the growing number of transactions with international agencies, it became mandatory to establish a section for handling that business. Unfortunately, since its functions were not clearly suited to any one existing division, it was made semi-independent, subject to the direction of both the political and economic divisions.

There were other problems as well. The placement of cultural affairs within the political division was not successful since it had no functional reason for being there. Organization by function did not

---

[22] Jon Rosenbaum, "A Critique of the Brazilian Foreign Service," *The Journal of Developing Areas,* April 1968, p. 378.

provide for a planning body that could be easily coordinated with the other divisions.[23] In addition, members of the key political and economic divisions were also assigned the routine tasks of border demarcation, diplomatic receptions, and passport issuance.[24]

In 1961, fifteen years after the first serious organizational-reform study was issued, a reorganization bill became law. It virtually did away with the functionalist approach. Geographic divisions were now the heart of the policy-making process, but a separate division for economic affairs was retained. The more routine matters were all given over to a separate Department of Administration.[25]

Quite possibly the most significant change for Itamaraty was the new power given to the secretary-general. In the past, his job was purely of an administrative nature, leaving the foreign minister free to deal with policy matters. Under the new law, the secretary-general became involved directly in making policy. A Secretariat of Foreign Affairs, composed of the secretary-general and the four chiefs of the geographic and economics divisions, was established and it was given responsibility for making and coordinating policy. As a result, the foreign minister became largely dependent on the senior professional diplomat—the secretary-general—for advice on substance and procedure.[26]

But structural reorganization is not the only key to Itamaraty's hold on foreign policy. During the last fifteen years there have been no less than thirteen foreign ministers. (The U.S., by contrast, has had five, including Secretary Kissinger.) This rapid turnover reflects, in part, the turbulence of Brazil's post-Vargas politics, but in any case, short tenures of office are not conducive to lasting influence on policy.

Further, nine of the last thirteen ministers were not professional diplomats.[27] Nor were they selected for the job because of their knowledge of foreign affairs (though most had at least a passing acquaintance with the subject). They were chosen because they were powerful politicians, often leaders of their own political parties. In Brazilian

---

[23] *Evolução do Ministério das Relações Exteriores* (Rio de Janeiro: Fundação Getúlio Vargas, n.d.), pp. 178-180; *Jornal do Brasil* (Rio de Janeiro), 22 September 1963, p. 21.

[24] *Itamaraty* (Rio de Janeiro), 15 February 1957, pp. 10-11. (*Itamaraty* was a monthly published by the Foreign Ministry.)

[25] *Jornal do Brasil* (Rio de Janeiro), 22 September 1963, p. 21.

[26] *Jornal do Brasil* (Rio de Janeiro), 21 May 1961, p. 4.

[27] The four, including the last two foreign ministers, were active foreign service officers from whom the foreign ministry had nothing to fear.

politics, especially before 1964, the multi-party system created the need for party coalitions to form a majority. Since the foreign ministry is one of the more prestigious posts, it was usually given to a man who could bring a considerable amount of political support to the ruling regime. Even under the military, civilian politicians have continued to occupy the post, and Costa e Silva's appointment of Magalhães Pinto, the powerful and popular governor of Minas Gerais, was designed primarily to attract the support of moderate-conservative civilian groups.

Finally, in his direct relations with Itamaraty, the foreign minister does not ordinarily select the secretary-general or the divisional chiefs. These choices are made for him by a promotion committee composed of senior diplomats. Even if the minister did choose on his own, his choice (by law) would be limited to professional diplomats. (The American secretary of state may appoint outsiders to the department's top positions.) Moreover, the foreign minister does not directly consult with his "assistant secretaries" but receives their policy recommendations through the secretary-general.[28]

Itamaraty and the Business Community

Itamaraty, despite its reputation, is not completely aloof; indeed, it has found working with others quite useful for its purposes. The business community, with its various associations, is the most important private "collaborator."[29] The business associations rarely exert direct, uninvited pressure on Itamaraty. The foreign office, on its own initiative, has sought their assistance by inviting them to formal discussions on economic matters of mutual interest—such as expanded trade with Eastern Europe.[30]

---

[28] Foreign Minister San Thiago Dantas, for example, called together the heads of mission for the East European countries for an informal session on future policy in the area. The novelty of this approach was duly reported in the press. *Jornal do Brasil* (Rio de Janeiro), 21 February 1962, p. 4; 22 February 1962, p. 3.

[29] San Thiago Dantas, foreign minister under João Goulart, once invited trade union officials for lunch at the ministry and encouraged them to pass foreign policy resolutions at their conventions. That action was deeply resented by the diplomats and was never repeated by subsequent foreign ministers.

[30] *Jornal do Brasil* (Rio de Janeiro), 10 April 1962, p. 8. It is perhaps significant that the only suggestion reported out of the meeting in April 1962 was Itamaraty's proposal to form a trade corporation similar to the French National Center for Foreign Trade. It would have been composed of private and government personnel, and would have dealt largely with socialist countries. What is important is that the foreign ministry used this discussion to add legitimacy to its trade promotion schemes, and not to learn anything from the business community.

Itamaraty also works with other government agencies when it is in its interest. In 1960, on the recommendation of Itamaraty, President Kubitschek created a Council of Foreign Trade. Its members included the secretary-general and the chief of the Economics Division from Itamaraty, plus the ministers of finance and labor. The council was ostensibly to act as a coordinator of all Brazilian foreign trade policy, but according to insiders, its real purpose was to give Itamaraty the central role in trade promotion. Apparently, senior Itamaraty officials felt the ministry's part had been too small in the international sugar and coffee conferences held the previous year.[31]

Itamaraty and the Military

Probably Itamaraty's most sensitive task in domestic diplomacy has been the maintenance of its relations with the military. The goal has been, of course, to keep good relations with the armed forces, while at the same time keeping firm control of foreign policy making. Itamaraty's success, especially since 1964, has been mixed. The foreign office-armed forces relationship will be examined at greater length below,[32] but one recent incident illuminates Itamaraty's problem. In October 1967, after a meeting of the military-dominated National Security Council, it was decided that the foreign office should be removed from any policy-making role in atomic development. The foreign ministry's sole duty would be to act as principal agent in the international negotiations concerning nuclear energy; but this would not include participation in the decisions made regarding the nation's negotiating position. In the meantime, basic policy would be developed by the minister of mines and energy, a post usually held by a military officer.[33]

The Men and Women of Itamaraty

Given its relative success in maintaining control of Brazilian foreign policy, what kind of policy does the foreign office advocate? The answer to that depends, in part, on the type of person drawn to the foreign service.

[31] *Jornal do Brasil* (Rio de Janeiro), 5 November 1959, pp. 5 and 10; and 6 November 1959, p. 11.
[32] See below, pp. 92-93.
[33] *Jornal do Brasil* (Rio de Janeiro), 8 October 1967, p. 6.

Itamaraty's critics have long charged it with assuming aristocratic airs because of its selection of young diplomats from the wealthy, established, white families of Rio de Janeiro. Most critics feel, in addition, that if Brazil is ever to have a "popular, democratic foreign policy" (to use the catchwords of the left), radical changes in recruitment have to be made. The ministry's defenders argue that selection is based on merit alone and has nothing to do with family connection (even though one estimate is that at least 10 percent of Itamaraty's personnel have a father, brother, or son in the service).[34] Nevertheless, admission into the Instituto Rio-Branco (which offers two years of training for the junior diplomat) is dependent on passing examinations, and nothing else.

In a sense, critic and apologist are talking past each other; what they both say is empirically correct. Rio's upper-middle class does dominate the foreign ministry, and they do so because of their superior educational background. It *is* an aristocracy in the classic sense of the word: rule of the best.

In order to pass the entrance exam, one must be well educated, and to be well educated costs money. Brazilian public universities are not nearly equal in quality to the private schools, much less to American universities. Therefore, only a few can afford to send their children to schools which can give them the proper preparation.[35]

So much is obvious, but why is it Rio's elite in particular that dominates Itamaraty? Since the eighteenth century, the city of Rio de Janeiro has been *the* outward looking city in Brazil; it was the political capital and principal seaport. That meant its elite would naturally assume the business of contacts with foreigners. It is Rio then that has the people who are most fluent in languages and who have had experience living abroad, including study at the foreign school. All of these factors then have given Rio the edge in the foreign ministry, and this is likely to continue even though the capital is now Brasilia.

Attempts have been made to alter the regional bias, but with limited results. Until 1958, the foreign service examinations were given only in Rio de Janeiro. Naturally this imposed an added burden on any nonresident. Kubitschek ordered additional test centers in São Paulo,

---

[34] Rosenbaum, "A Critique," p. 379.

[35] According to Rosenbaum, 43 percent of the diplomats active between 1964 and 1966 were born in the city of Rio de Janeiro. The next largest contributors, the states of São Paulo and Minas Gerais, each had 8 percent. In addition, many officers not born in Rio were Rio residents at the time of admission to the foreign service. Ibid., p. 384.

Belo Horizonte, Porto Alegre, and Recife. This, however, seems to have made no difference. It is true that in the first year of the new examining centers' operation, some 48 percent of the examinees were from outside Rio de Janeiro, but they managed to win only 20 percent of the openings in the first-year class at the Rio-Branco Institute. One reason for this is a valuable pre-exam preparatory course offered only in Rio. Scholarships for this course are available but they are small; only the wealthiest applicants from outside the old capital can afford to take the course.[36]

Thus there is good reason to believe that the foreign office will continue to be dominated by residents from Rio de Janeiro. In addition, those who entered the ministry before 1958 will continue to hold the positions of power for another two decades; most Brazilian diplomats remain with Itamaraty until retirement.[37]

Discipline at Itamaraty

Discovering the reasons behind Itamaraty's perspective on the world is not simply a matter of uncovering recruitment patterns. For one thing, though the social backgrounds of those in the foreign service are similar, political opinions are diverse. More important is the effect of the foreign policy "fraternity's" views on the junior officer. The senior officers of Itamaraty like to characterize the agency as a club. The club has a definite point of view as well as a set of very precise rules. Its members are not hesitant about instilling them in the junior officers.

It is also a club with a club. Itamaraty is a strictly hierarchical organization with tight discipline. When decisions are made, there is no dissent, especially from the younger officers, and there are no news leaks or sudden resignations with indiscreet disclosures to the public. It is, in short, very much like a European foreign office and very much unlike the U.S. Department of State.[38]

---

[36] There are exceptions. Roberto Campos came from a relatively poor family in Mato Grosso. He studied for the priesthood on a scholarship in a provincial school, but changed his mind about the church and took and passed the entrance exam for the Rio-Branco Institute.

[37] *Jornal do Brasil* (Rio de Janeiro), 13 August 1959; Rosenbaum, "A Critique," p. 384.

[38] According to Rosenbaum only one career officer resigned between 1958 and 1966. Rosenbaum, "A Critique," p. 380.

The World View of Itamaraty

The system of recruitment and discipline, plus the institutional aura of respect for tradition and the "spirit of Itamaraty," has produced a distinct foreign office outlook on international affairs. It is nationalist, but more pragmatic than romantic.[39] It is oriented toward Europe and not America.[40] It emphasizes preservation of good relations with old friends, but not at the expense of making new ones. It entails a desire for a larger Brazilian role on the world scene, but it does not exaggerate the nation's present prospects for world power. Grand but impractical schemes are not in the picture.

The Foreign Ministry thinks of itself as an institution which carries on in "a spirit of tradition without moss." It is also very self-assured about its views and is certain that it knows best when it comes to Brazil's foreign affairs.[41]

This outlook can be seen best by a comparison of two professional diplomats who served very different regimes as foreign minister. The first, Araujo Castro, served during the most radical period of the Goulart regime—August 1963–April 1964. The second, Vasco Leitão da Cunha, led Itamaraty during the year after the April 1964 revolution. Both men expressed viewpoints which hardly differed, although the regimes they served most certainly did.

In a newspaper interview, Castro made a carefully balanced statement which informed readers that Brazil was going through an ideological phase which other nations had passed through decades earlier. He said that

> the extreme right in Brazil is kilometers to the right of the Pentagon, and the extreme left is kilometers to the left of the Kremlin. If some of our more extreme ideologies of the left and of the right had influence on the diplomatic action of the USSR and the United States—which fortunately they don't—

---

[39] One should not overstress the "Young-Turk-tamed" theme. Jon Rosenbaum found that 68 percent of students considering the service were doing so because it promised *a boa vida* (the good life). Another 20 percent liked the idea of foreign travel. Rosenbaum's sample size was twenty-five. Ibid., footnote, p. 385.

[40] Itamaraty has not hesitated to clash with the U.S. on matters considered important to Brazil: It opposed participation of U.S. technicians in a Brazilian oil-finding venture in Bolivia's Robore district. It was against American assistance in Brazil's nuclear development and was apparently willing to whip up nationalist sentiment over the issue. *Jornal do Brasil* (Rio de Janeiro), 15 August 1967, p. 6.

[41] Rosenbaum, "A Critique," pp. 380 and 390.

then the world long ago would have turned into a heap of ruins.[42]

And he concluded: "A foreign policy, to be truly independent, has to be independent from pressures of immaturity and radicalism." [43] This was a clear warning to the left (and, to a much lesser extent, to the far right) that militant slogans were not welcome at Itamaraty.

In an interview with the magazine, *Manchete,* Castro set down the fundamental themes of Brazil's foreign policy: development, disarmament, and decolonialization. In the meantime, he said, the position of "neutralism or non-alignment" for Brazil was unacceptable, for such catchwords were irrelevant to the previously announced goals. He made clear that "Brazil is looking for an authentic position, suitable to its problems . . . and refuses to place its foreign policy in impractical positions. . . ." [44]

His successor, Vasco Leitão da Cunha, though serving an entirely different regime, supported a similar set of policies. Development, disarmament, and decolonialization were not repudiated. The only new policy was a specific verbal commitment to the West. But Leitão da Cunha's declaration of allegiance to the West did not mean a diminution in contacts with the East: "We want good and honest business with all peoples of the world. . . . everyone avidly pursues markets all over the world. And in this all the world's governments coincide, capitalist, socialist, Marxist-Leninist, et cetera. The great reality in the world these days is trade. Everyone wants to trade." [45]

Common threads run through these statements. Both men were intent on trimming away ideological excess. Both dwelt on the practical needs of Brazil and how foreign policy should meet those needs. Both represent the mainstream of Itamaraty thought and practice: the acceptance of change and adjustment when necessary, but a refusal to approve radical shifts.

Itamaraty's Problems and Prospects

Itamaraty has dominated foreign policy in the past, but will it be able to in the future? If so, it must solve a number of critical problems.

---

[42] *Itamaraty*, January 1964, pp. 9-10.

[43] Ibid., p. 10.

[44] Ibid., p. 12.

[45] Quoted in *Revista Brasileira de Política Internacional*, September 1964, p. 593.

The first of these is a lack of personnel. The service is very small,[46] and although over the last decade the authorized number of professionals has increased from 465 to 868, the actual number has gone up much more slowly. Thus, Itamaraty does not have enough men of ambassadorial rank to staff its embassies.[47] At the home office, there are similar shortages. For example, in 1968 three officers (including two junior diplomats) were responsible for eighteen countries plus the Vatican. Until 1962, one man in the Economics Division kept track of Europe, Africa, Asia, and Oceania.[48] The problem is aggravated by the fact that senior diplomats, in addition to their regular desk duties, are called upon to staff study groups devoted to research and policy recommendations on a wide range of subjects, including trade promotion, atomic energy, and ministry reform.[49]

A second problem flows from the first: the foreign office lacks special expertise. Together with the fact that a majority at Itamaraty are proud of being generalists and political experts rather than narrow-gauge technicians, the lack of numbers inhibits specialization. A diplomat's assignment is usually for two years, and it is rare when any two consecutive assignments are in the same region of the world. Furthermore, within the headquarters geographic divisions the general rule is that one officer does not take responsibility for a particular set of countries. Instead, each diplomat may freely move within a geographic division on an ad hoc basis. After two years he may move on to another division or, more usually, a field assignment.

The result of all this is foreign service officers with strikingly varied careers. A former chief of the Western European division had never held a European post when he took over the division; his experience had been entirely in Latin America. Another chief of the old West European and African division had to visit Africa after taking his position because he had never been there before.[50]

---

[46] There were 525 officers in 1966 compared to the State Department's 7,000. Rosenbaum, "A Critique," footnote, p. 379.

[47] By 1968 four embassies in Africa alone were unfilled as well as five consulates. *Jornal do Brasil* (Rio de Janeiro), 30 July 1967, p. 4. See also *Jornal do Brasil*, 21 May 1961, p. 4.

[48] *Jornal do Brasil* (Rio de Janeiro), 12 April 1961, p. 4.

[49] *Jornal do Brasil* (Rio de Janeiro), 21 May 1961, p. 4.

[50] *Jornal do Brasil* (Rio de Janeiro), 9 November 1961, p. 4.

This approach causes a certain amount of haphazardness. Heavy responsibility may be given to someone who is not acquainted with an area's problems, although his procedural training may be excellent.

Not everyone, however, is pleased with things as they are. Indeed, a small, probably growing, and relatively aggressive group within the ministry has steadily lobbied for more specialized personnel, especially in economics.[51] The "modernizers" (many were trained in the United States) have contended for nearly two decades that a developing country's central concern is, after all, development, and a rational foreign economic policy is crucial to attain that goal. Unless Itamaraty takes the lead with qualified officers, it will either lose control of the most important substantive part of foreign policy to others or Brazil will be needlessly handicapped by bad economic policy. The generalists (they call themselves "political specialists") have fought back, disparaging specialization in general and economics in particular.[52]

The economists, however, have made some gains. Decree Law 69, signed by Castelo Branco in November 1966, permitted the foreign office, for the first time, to hire outside the foreign service in order to fill overseas specialist positions.[53] How often that option has been used, though, is not known to the author.

The key problem is the training given to incoming diplomats. The Rio-Branco Institute provides junior officers two years of post-university education, and thus could provide a good opportunity for advanced work in foreign policy. But that is not now the case. Although the work load is heavy, the emphasis remains on law, languages, and diplomatic history. Little attention is given to economics or any other social science. Furthermore, the library is inadequate and students are taught by a part-time faculty. Research on contemporary foreign policy problems is not encouraged.[54] Finally, there is no provision for further training at the mid-career level. Suggestions on how to overcome this

---

[51] Rosenbaum estimates that the group comprises 10 percent of the foreign service and dates the opening of the controversy sometime in the 1950s. Rosenbaum, "A Critique," p. 387.

[52] Ibid., pp. 386-387. The modernizers have fought other battles. For example, they have tried to downgrade the foreign language requirement in order to make room for more economics.

[53] Ibid., pp. 379-380.

[54] Ibid., pp. 382-383 and 385-386. It must be remembered that political science, and especially international relations, as taught in the United States, may be as abstruse and as irrelevant to the practice of American diplomacy as a Brazilian course in international law.

are constantly circulating, but the ministry operates within a tight budget, and no program has been set up.

Itamaraty will be working with an increasing handicap if changes are not made. For one thing, the rest of the Brazilian bureaucracy is beginning to catch up, and the foreign ministry can no longer count upon the deference paid to it in the past. In the past few years, certain ministries, especially finance, have not hesitated to move into foreign areas that Itamaraty seemed ill equipped to handle.

There are recent signs that Itamaraty is fully aware of the threat, and has made some effort to overcome this deficiency. In fall 1973, when Delfim Neto, minister of finance, turned over to Itamaraty tariff negotiations with the European Economic Community, the foreign ministry seized the opportunity by sending a team led by the secretary-general. Three months later, the team had concluded highly favorable agreements on soluble coffee and cocoa butter without making any significant (and expected) concessions on Brazilian requirements to carry goods in Brazilian bottoms.[55]

The Working Style of Itamaraty

Closely linked to the problem of specialists is the argument over planning. In 1960 an economic planning unit was established in Itamaraty.[56] In 1967 a similar body was organized for planning political policy. Naturally, both have been objects of considerable debate within the ministry. The modernizers argue that a coherent and practical foreign policy can only be designed by men who are removed from the daily routine of the foreign office. The absence of planning in the past is reflected in the Brazilian penchant for ad hoc solutions, determined on the basis of the time-honored *palpite* (roughly, an inspired hunch) rather than by careful calculation. Nothing is anticipated; nothing precise is posited for the ministry to achieve.

The modernizers' critics point out the problems in central planning: Planning and analysis is already done within each division. Thus, the introduction of central planning would result in much duplication of effort. Planning, especially of the long-range variety, is an exercise in futility since policy can only be stated in the most general of terms.

---

[55] *Latin America* (London), 31 August 1973, p. 277, and 14 December 1973, p. 394.
[56] *Jornal do Brasil* (Rio de Janeiro), 22 September 1963.

In addition, if the planning function were removed from the working divisions, confusion would result, and some divisions would be left without work since analysis is their reason for being.[57]

So far, each division does what it wants to do in the planning area with much of the actual research left to junior diplomats. The policy-planning bodies are left, meanwhile, to operate on their own, quite removed from the rest of Itamaraty. The ministry remains, in the words of one insider, "a one-legged animal. It only has an operational leg and does not have an intelligence and planning leg." [58]

If Itamaraty refuses to become a three-legged beast, what will become of it? One might assume a similar outcome in the case of the specialists: others will do the job for Itamaraty. In the case of policy planning this has to a large extent already come to pass. Within the armed forces, a number of senior officers with advanced educations have for a decade set about the task of elaborating an integrated doctrine of development, security, and foreign policy. And it is to the military we must now turn our attention.

The Military and Foreign Policy

The military today is no small factor in the foreign policy-making process in Brazil. Historian John Johnson has said of the 1930 revolution that it was the event which propelled "the armed forces into the center of Brazilian politics, and the locus of power has resided in them ever since." [59] He goes on to say: "More significantly, perhaps, within the last decade the representatives of the armed forces again have become increasingly prone to take public positions on policy conflicts rather than being content to arbitrate the differences that arise from civilian debate." [60] This is certainly nothing new for a continent which literally pioneered the techniques and nuances of modern military politics. But it is relatively new for Brazil's armed forces, whose earlier role has been described by officer and civilian alike as "moderator" of the political system.

---

[57] This is especially true for Itamaraty's North American division, which must allow major decisions to be made by the president and the foreign minister.
[58] Quoted in Rosenbaum, "A Critique," p. 387.
[59] John J. Johnson, *The Military and Society in Latin America* (Stanford, Calif.: Stanford University Press, 1964), p. 206.
[60] Ibid., p. 206. Alfred Stepan, *The Military in Politics: Changing Patterns in Brazil* (Princeton, N.J.: Princeton University Press, 1971), considerably amplifies and refines Johnson's findings. See especially chapters 5 and 6.

Military involvement in Brazilian politics is not a simple matter of command and obey. The Brazilian military is not a monolith: there have been three major factions within the armed forces in recent years. Each has its viewpoints on policy and its own techniques for getting them implemented. Junior officers, especially, have mastered the finer shades of insubordination—including publicity—in order to make their views felt. In this respect the Brazilian military contrasts sharply with Itamaraty.

In order to understand the complex nature of Brazilian military politics, it is first necessary to trace the development of factionalism—a factionalism based on deep differences of opinion on issues that have affected relations with the United States directly and indirectly.[61]

Although the Brazilian military [62] has been divided before on various questions, the present cleavages first became visible in 1950. In the late 1940s an intense debate broke out between two senior officers over petroleum policy: Should the United States be asked to assist in exploration and exploitation or should Brazil go it alone? The focal point of the discussion was shifted to the Clube Militar where the issue soon became part of the organization's electoral process.[63] Unlike previous Clube contests, candidates emerged with distinct and heated points of view on national issues. And the nationalists triumphed in the May 1950 elections.[64] Newly elected Clube president General

---

[61] The political activists within the military are a minority of the officer corps. Nevertheless, it is the men with ideas who have shaped the armed forces role in politics and not the "pure professional," who wishes to remain outside the political arena. One important activist general has stated: "Military activists for or against the government are always a minority. If a military group wants to overthrow a government they need to convince the great majority of officers who are either strict legalists or simply nonactivists. Activists do not wish to risk bloodshed or military splits, so they wait until a consensus has developed." Quoted in Stepan, *The Military in Politics,* p. 97.

[62] The military in this context means the army, which has an overwhelming amount of power compared to the other services. The navy has not been crucial in matters of high politics since the unsuccessful naval revolt of 1893.

[63] The Clube Militar, founded in 1887, is ostensibly a recreational and mutual benefit society for commissioned officers of all services. In fact, it was founded so that the military could debate such issues as slavery and republicanism. In the 1920s the Clube became a forum of *tenentismo,* a program of reform espoused by junior officers. During the Vargas years, 1930-1945, the Clube was kept under close scrutiny (which is also the case today) and political expression was minimal. See Johnson, *Military and Society,* pp. 219-220; Stepan, *The Military in Politics,* pp. 44-45.

[64] The "nationalist" candidate, General Estillac Leal, may have greatly improved his chances by also favoring increased military salaries. The staunch left-wing officers in his entourage, nevertheless, believed the election was a mandate for

Estillac Leal proceeded to pack the organization's directorate with highly nationalist junior officers who favored such measures as massive redistribution of wealth and state intervention in the economy to spur industrialization.[65]

Two other events further deepened the divisions within the officer corps. First, Getúlio Vargas assumed the presidency, confident that the nationalist faction of the armed forces would keep him in power. To further solidify his position, Vargas appointed Estillac Leal war minister, over the objections of anti-nationalist officers.[66]

The second major event that served to crystallize the military groups was United States involvement in the Korean conflict. An unsigned article appeared in the July 1950 issue of the Clube's new nationalist journal, *Revista do Clube Militar,* accusing the United States of intervention in a civil war which it had instigated. The article further recommended that Brazil remain strictly neutral on the issue.[67]

The reaction was immediate. Nelson Werneck Sodré, then a junior officer on the *Revista* staff, records in his memoirs an impressive list of protest letters from officers stationed in every corner of Brazil.[68] The high command was no happier and suspended the publication of the *Revista* in mid-December 1950.[69] Two weeks later, most of the Clube's officers, including the editor of the *Revista,* were transferred to distant garrison posts.[70]

---

their foreign policy views. Ronald Schneider, *The Political System of Brazil: Emergence of a "Modernizing" Authoritarian Regime, 1964-1970* (New York: Columbia University Press, 1971), p. 60.

[65] See the *Revista do Clube Militar,* July 1950, especially its editorial, "O Significado de uma Vitória," pp. 3-4, which stresses the military's role in defending the national patrimony against foreign interests.

[66] Skidmore, *Politics in Brazil,* p. 104; Schneider, *The Political System of Brazil,* pp. 59-60.

[67] "Crónica Internacional: Considerações sobre a Guerra na Coréia," *Revista do Clube Militar,* July 1950, pp. 75-80. See also (General) Nelson Werneck Sodré, *Memórias de um Soldado* (Rio de Janeiro: Civilização Brasileira, 1967), pp. 310-320. General Werneck Sodré, a Marxist historian, was a member of the Clube's directorate, and although he still claims that he does not know who wrote the article (it was signed Captain X), some suspect him of authorship. See p. 321 of his memoirs.

[68] One dated 31 October stated in part: ". . . it is strange that our *Revista* . . . has published under its auspices an article . . . which outlines such a course in the present international emergency. . . . I believe, Mr. President Estillac Leal, that this attitude on the part of our *Revista* needs to be reconsidered, as well as the . . . liberty of thought among the members of the *Clube Militar.*" The author: Humberto de Castelo Branco. Quoted in Werneck Sodré, *Memórias,* pp. 317-318.

[69] Skidmore, *Politics in Brazil,* p. 105.

[70] Werneck Sodré, *Memórias,* pp. 348-349.

But before the crackdown, the nationalists fired another round at the United States. Another "Capitão X" article appeared, denouncing the attempt to "give away" national resources to foreign oil trusts. Other similar statements followed before the review's suspension, and six more like-minded articles appeared after the suspension was lifted in April 1951.[71]

Two years after the controversy began, an aroused and organized group of anti-leftist members of the Clube Militar defeated the nationalists and their incumbent candidate, General Estillac Leal, by a nearly two-to-one majority.[72]

The conclusion of the Korean War and the passage of nationalist petroleum legislation in 1951 did not bring the politically minded officers together. Clube elections continued to be bitterly contested, with the moderates winning in 1952 and again in 1954 and then losing the next three elections. But win or lose, the themes never changed: the nationalists kept up their attack on the *entreguistas,* while their opponents repeated their warnings about a Jacobin-Communist threat to the Brazilian way of life.[73]

There was one important development in those years, however. The more conservative officers, after repeated defeats in the Clube Militar elections, broke into two camps: the moderates—who were soon labelled the Sorbonne group [74]—led by Castelo Branco and the more conservative elements who had their roots in the Cruzada Democrática. The moderates maintained a pro-United States stance, but did not scorn the notion of developmental nationalism. The conservatives—often tagged the *linha dura* (hard line)—stressed a rigid domestic anti-communism, and had little to say about economic development.[75]

---

[71] Representative articles were: R. Descartes Garcia Paula, "Petróleo e Minas Estratégicas," *Revista do Clube Militar,* April 1951, pp. 58-74; Captain Ernesto Gurgel do Amaral, "O Petróleo é Nosso mas os Dólares são para os Americanos e Ingleses," *Revista do Clube Militar,* July-August 1951, pp. 37-40.

[72] The Clube president had earlier met defeat at the hands of the moderate officers when he was forced to resign (March 1952). For a favorable treatment of that officer and his views, see Skidmore, *Politics in Brazil,* pp. 104-106.

[73] Most of the activist officers in the 1950s controversies faced each other a decade later in March 1964. Schneider, *The Political System of Brazil,* pp. 60-61. The nationalists were able to win the 1956-1960 elections (they were narrowly defeated in 1962) because of friendly war ministers like Marshall Henrique Teixeira Lott.

[74] The label refers to the fact that most of those officers graduated at the top of their class and have attended foreign military schools, especially the Ecole de Guerre in France.

[75] The Cruzada was the original core of very conservative officers who organized themselves in order to challenge the nationalists in 1950.

75

Thus, by 1964 three military factions had evolved, and two of them are still very much a part of Brazilian politics. With this background, we can now focus on each major faction in the military. Who are they, what kind of power do they have, how do they use their influence, and what positions do they hold on Brazil's foreign policy? It is also necessary to pinpoint the roles they play in the policy-making process and to determine if they will continue to influence that process in the future.

One caveat is in order at this point: although the political activists among the officers tend to have fallen into three (now two) factions, the latter term must not be mistaken to mean a tightly knit group of like-minded men holding membership cards in a very exclusive club. As one observer shrewdly suggested:

> Division into sharply differentiated groups of "hard liners" and the "Sorbonne," useful as it is for understanding the dialectics of the Castelo Branco period, imposes a rigidity that often did not exist in reality. To some extent, both of these groupings are more a state of mind than a structured clique. Moreover, many Brazilian officers conform to neither of these ideal types but manifest a good deal of ambivalence in their attitudes and ambiguity in their positions.[76]

Furthermore, officers have been known to switch positions entirely or drop out of military politics altogether, and the factions themselves differ in structure. The Sorbonne group is relatively cohesive, with its members often working together on a regular, face-to-face basis. This cohesiveness is primarily a consequence of the commonly shared, intensely felt experience of modern warfare. The left-wing nationalists, on the other hand, were a much more amorphous group with little ability for coordinated action.

The Nationalists

Nationalism, in some form, is part of the ideological baggage of any army. This is obvious, but it does provide a case for examining the left-wing nationalists who otherwise have been in eclipse since 1964.[77]

---

[76] Schneider, *The Political System of Brazil,* p. 144.

[77] A total of 112 officers were immediately retired after the April revolt; others were expelled during the following year. Still others were told they would not receive another promotion. Stepan, *The Military in Politics,* p. 223.

It is true that those officers associated with Getúlio Vargas, and later, João Goulart, were involuntarily retired. But their views have proved so infectious in the past, there is reason to believe that left-wing nationalism will return under a later, more tolerant regime.

In Brazil, furthermore, the variant of nationalism that couples desire for fundamental reform with love of country and fear of external threat has flourished in the military (especially the army) since the last days of the empire.[78] In the 1920s, a very pronounced example of this type of nationalism surfaced among junior officers who were tired of rule by the coffee planters and demanded rapid change through industrialization and political reform, especially in public administration.[79]

The young nationalist officers of 1950 were able to draw on a long tradition of reform spearheaded by the military. What did these junior officers have in common besides their belief in autarky and a complementary suspicion of the United States?

In the first place, the bulk of the officers in the nationalist movement were junior officers. They also were pro-Vargas and eagerly supported his return to power in 1950. Not surprisingly many of the nationalists were from Vargas's home state, Rio Grande do Sul.[80] Those officers who were not from that southernmost state received their introduction to politics in the Third Army, based in the state's capital, Porto Alegre.[81] More importantly, few, if any, of these officers served in the Brazilian Expeditionary Force, which formed part of the American

---

[78] Officers held lively debates on issues such as slavery in Brazil. See Haring, *Empire in Brazil*, p. 102.

[79] See Robert Alexander, "Brazilian 'Tenentismo,' " *Hispanic American Historical Review*, May 1956, pp. 229-242. It is somewhat ironic that the *tenente* leaders like Eduardo Gomes and Juracy Malgahães would so vigorously oppose the nationalist officers of the 1950s. Gomes was the first honorary president of the Cruzada Democrática.

[80] Prominent left-wing nationalists included Werneck Sodré and Goulart's war minister, General Jair Dantas Ribeiro.

[81] The Third Army's political radicalism was widely known and commented upon in Brazil. Militarily it was also the most powerful because of its closeness to Argentina. Goulart ensured the Third Army's loyalty by regularly staffing it with the most nationalist officers available. But previously that army had proved valuable to left-wing politicians. In 1930 it joined Getúlio Vargas's revolt against the government, and in 1961 it demanded that Goulart be allowed to succeed Quadros despite the objections of the chiefs of the military services. In 1963, a right-wing plot in which Brazilian and Argentine guerrillas were to provoke a border skirmish which would occupy the Third Army while the other armies carried out a coup against Goulart was detailed in the leftist *Última Hora* (Rio de Janeiro), 5 June 1963. See also Stepan, *The Military in Politics*, pp. 27 and 96.

Fifth Army in northern Italy during World War II, or attended foreign military schools. Their careers were, in short, Brazilian-based.

This type of officer, not surprisingly, espoused a highly charged nationalism mixed with a derivative (and, to purists, sometimes alarmingly vague) Marxism. But whatever its ultimate ideological sources, the master premise of their ideology remained distrust of foreign investors coupled with an extravagant enthusiasm for Brazil's natural resources. General Valério Braga stated it succinctly: ". . . to give the foreign trusts the right to exploit our oil would constitute the monstrous crime of treason to our country." [82] But nationalist officers were not merely content to list the virtues of a state oil monopoly. In addition, they lobbied vigorously for state monopolies over electrical energy and atomic minerals.[83]

The most ardent nationalists went even further. Nelson Werneck Sodré, their most prolific spokesman, has written extensively on the postwar world. He has consistently argued that the cold war is an American device to divide the world into two camps: the "Christian West" and the "Communist East." The adversary relationship with the Communist nations permits the Americans to station troops on every continent and turn European allies into satellites. Latin America is intended to be the source of huge profits to help pay for the United States "defense" system. Finally, in rejecting Soviet offers of peaceful coexistence, the United States makes World War III inevitable. In short, "North American imperialism, which economically and politically oppresses the dependent nations, constitutes a major threat to world peace." [84]

A good deal of Werneck Sodré's analysis is, of course, familiar to even the most casual reader of the *World Marxist Review,* but it is the best organized extant sample of the larger nationalist world view. (At the same time, it should be noted that few left-wing officers are as extreme in their opinions as Werneck Sodré.) [85]

---

[82] General Valério Braga, "Importância do Monopólio Estatal do Petróleo para o Progresso do Brasil," *Revista do Clube Militar* (no month given), 1957, p. 38.

[83] See, for example, Naval Captain Primo Nunes de Andrade, "Os Militares no Empolgante Batalha do Desenvolvimento," *Revista do Clube Militar,* June-September 1956, pp. 17-20.

[84] Werneck Sodré, *Memórias,* pp. 332-333.

[85] Marshall Osvino Alves, the self-styled "people's general," was an exception, and was one of the few military men who lost their political rights in April 1964. Schneider, *The Political System of Brazil,* pp. 90 and 128.

Nevertheless, the nationalists did move beyond the old question of foreign exploitation of oil resources. They supported Quadros's independent foreign policy. Marshall Osvino Alves, in 1962 commander of the powerful First Army, announced that he would back the new policy, which he classified as a move that "the government considered necessary in order to attain for Brazil a position of independence. . . ." [86]

On a very few occasions, the nationalists acted as a body. In April 1961, risking censure, the nationalist directorate of the Clube Militar sent a telegram of congratulations to President Quadros on his announcement of the resumption of relations with the Soviet Union.[87] Nationalist army officers, however, generally proved inept at influencing government policy [88] or turning the Brazilian army into the "people in uniform"—one of their favorite slogans. Nevertheless, they tried.

The basic strategy was to obtain control of the Clube Militar and use its facilities to expound nationalist doctrines. The Clube, they announced in 1950, was not a society for recreation or for mutual benefit; it was a "vigilant and active organ," fighting for "the consolidation of our economic independence." [89] They said that it was their primary duty to shape the opinions of the officer corps, "a homogeneous body of men whose spirit was unalterably and decidedly committed to the defense and progress of the country." [90]

Prominent left-wing politicians were invited to speak to senior officers at Clube headquarters in Rio. The topics of these talks proved invariably to be state ownership of minerals and the need for a profit remittance law. Nationalist junior officers also enrolled in the basic course offered by the Instituto Superior de Estudos Brasileiros, an organization dedicated to Marxist study of the "Brazilian reality." [91]

All of this "political socialization" meant a hundred officers or less got a smattering of classroom Marxism while many more were

[86] Osvino Alves, in a speech reported in the *Jornal do Brasil* (Rio de Janeiro), 29 May 1962, p. 3. *Última Hora* (Rio de Janeiro), 29 May 1962, p. 4, reported that, in the same speech, the general also vigorously denounced the rightists who, under the rubric of fighting communism, attempted to establish a dictatorship after the resignation of Jânio Quadros.

[87] Conservative War Minister Odílio Denys placed these officers under house arrest for forty-eight hours. See *Jornal do Brasil* (Rio de Janeiro), 5 April 1961, p. 4, and 26 April 1961, p. 4.

[88] The establishment of Petrobrás was an exception.

[89] "O Significado," pp. 3-4.

[90] Ibid., p. 4.

[91] The *Revista do Clube Militar*, no. 146 (no month given), 1957, lists ten officers who were selected by the Clube to attend the Curso Regular given by ISEB.

treated to articles and editorials announcing Brazil's greatness and the need to protect the national patrimony which assured that greatness.[92]

But organization remained the nationalists' weak point. Like their civilian comrades, they relied heavily on the assumption that they were already a vanguard of the awakened, invincible masses. This over-confidence was reflected in the leftist press: Batista de Paula, a columnist for *Última Hora,* was very enthusiastic about the "new armed forces." On one occasion he wrote:

> We ought to thank God that we have an advanced officer corps, enlightened and politically educated sergeants, and now even a body of officers composed of young men from all social classes.
> Here there are no *gorilas* to defend the reactionary interests, because the voice of the people is always louder in the barracks, on the bases, and on the ships.[93]

The nationalists also believed that control of the armed forces was assured if nationalist (or at least non-political, legalist) officers were in the major command positions.[94] But it was only paper strength. The nationalists did not have the political talent or the numbers to neutralize the power held by the divisional and regimental commanders of the widely dispersed Brazilian army, much less that held by the anti-Goulart governors of São Paulo, Minas Gerais, Guanabara, and Rio Grande do Sul, who controlled large, well-equipped state militias. Thus, the nationalists, despite possessing an ideology that capitalized on the mixture of love of country and fear of the foreigner that is traditional Brazilian nationalism, failed to win in 1964.

The Moderates

The moderate officers are the best organized and most articulate in the Brazilian military. Unlike the left-wing nationalists they have learned to work together as a group to achieve political ends. However, their

---

[92] Sample: "The truth is that Brazil cannot stop. It will have to accomplish its historic destiny, and by the end of the century it will become a great power. Then Brazil and her people will definitely be free and respected." From the *Revista do Clube Militar,* October-December 1960, pp. 2-3.

[93] Batista de Paula, from his regular military column, "Plantão Militar" in *Última Hora* (Rio de Janeiro), 10 July 1962, p. 11.

[94] These included the minister of war, the three armed-service chiefs, and the field commanders of the First and Third Armies (Rio de Janeiro and Porto Alegre).

political beliefs are not so obviously rooted in Brazilian history; this has left them vulnerable to nationalist charges of *entreguismo*.

The striking fact about the moderates is their highly similar career experiences. In chronological order: they served with the Brazilian Expeditionary Force (FEB) in World War II, they attended French and American military schools, they served on the faculty of the Escola Superior de Guerra (the National War College of Brazil), and they were with the army general staff—often for prolonged periods of time.[95]

Thus, a sample of one dozen politically active moderate officers turned up ten who served in the FEB, eight had been attached to the national war college, all had foreign training, and all had served on the general staff.[96] The shared experiences of wartime plus their advanced educations and their continued contact with each other at staff headquarters assured a high degree of self-confidence in themselves and each other, as well as a shared view of the world.

What political views have emerged from this cluster of commonly shared experiences? In foreign policy, FEB officers found that a close relationship with the U.S. could be mutually profitable.[97] Furthermore, these officers were enormously impressed by the contrast between the real power of the United States with its liberal democratic and capitalist ethos, and the impotence of Fascist Italy. Therefore, they considered

---

[95] This is in contrast to the leftist officers who served mostly with one of the field armies and had only brief stints at general headquarters. In addition, Alfred Stepan has found in his study of the FEB group that most graduated at the top of their class and then went into the most technical branch of the army, artillery. Stepan, *The Military in Politics*, pp. 238-239.

[96] Information on career backgrounds is available in the *Almanaque do Exército* (Rio de Janeiro: Ministério da Guerra, 1964). The officers selected on the basis of published political opinions were Humberto Castelo Branco, José Campos de Aração, Agusto Muniz de Aragão, Aurélio de Lyra Tavares, Carlos de Meira Mattos, Ademar de Queiroz, Nelson de Melo, Newton Foutoura, Nestor Penha Brasil and José Machado Lopes. Stepan selected ten officers who were judged to be influential in the Castelo Branco administration and found six had been in the FEB, nine had been connected with the ESG as students, seven had been on the staff of the Escola, all had graduated first in their class, and all had attended foreign military schools. The percentages for all line officers and pro-Goulart, nationalist generals were far lower. Stepan points out that the probability of these differences in percentage happening by chance is one in a thousand. Stepan, *The Military in Politics*, pp. 239-241.

[97] One FEB officer has stated: "In the war, the United States had to give us everything: food, clothes, equipment. After the war, we were less afraid of United States imperialism than other officers because we saw that the United States really helped us without strings attached." Quoted in Stepan, *The Military in Politics*, p. 242. One question comes to mind: why did the FEB officers not come to resent this utter dependence on the U.S.? It may be that any resentment was balanced by the genuine pride in the Brazilian division's fighting ability.

81

romantic nationalism, which ruled out cooperation with anyone, provincial, irrational, and damaging to Brazil's interest. The nationalists' heady rhetoric about Brazil struggling alone to greatness struck the moderates as implausible and as empty as Mussolini's vision of Italian grandeur.[98]

But by the mid-1950s they had gone beyond a simple distrust of romantic nationalism to an elaborately worked out doctrine of national security rooted in economic development and complemented by a well-focused foreign policy. Long-range as well as "current" objectives were defined, as were the concept of national power and the policies necessary to secure the objectives that had been established. Their work was heavily dependent on European geopolitical thinking, but it was also liberally sprinkled with references to Walter Lippmann, Harold Lasswell, and Hans Morganthau.[99]

The moderates' key doctrine of national security through economic development rested on the premise that Brazil was vulnerable to internal warfare and, therefore, international impotence as long as it remained underdeveloped. Overcoming this required a mixture of a strong, centralized state plus a vigorous and cooperative private sector. They also held that domestic turmoil was exacerbated by outsiders, principally the Soviet Union. Therefore, the United States, as leader of the Western alliance, is Brazil's natural ally.

But what specific set of policies would best serve the national security? General Carlos de Meira Mattos picked up where the theoretical geopoliticians usually leave off. Meira Mattos, who served in the FEB and was long attached to the general staff, has laid the foundation of the moderate officers' world view in a series of army-sponsored books and articles.[100]

---

[98] Ibid., p. 87.

[99] See General Golbery do Couto e Silva, *Planejamento Estratégico* (Rio de Janeiro: Biblioteca do Exército, 1955), and his *Geopolítica do Brasil* (Rio de Janeiro: Livraria José Olýmpio, 1967). An entire issue of *Revista Brasileira de Estudos Políticos,* Brazil's best journal of political science, was devoted to the subject of national security. See especially General Edmundo Domingues de Oliveira, "Segurança Nacional: Conceitos Fundamentais," in the *Revista,* July 1966, pp. 71-79. The best summary of this school of thought in English is in Schneider, *The Political System of Brazil,* pp. 246-248, and Stepan, *The Military in Politics,* pp. 178-183.

[100] Meira Mattos, besides being a prolific writer, was also a close friend of Castelo Branco, who gave him command of the Brazilian contingent in Santo Domingo, and then appointed him commander of the military police in Brasilia. See Schneider, *The Political System of Brazil,* pp. 101, 147, 184, 239, and 252, for highlights of his career.

In the typically systematic fashion of the FEB officers, Meira Mattos asserted that the parameters of Brazil's foreign policy were: (1) the historic roots of the nation's formation, (2) its geographic placement, and (3) the authentic aspirations of its people. He then listed three historic roots: First, Brazil was founded by Portugal, which gives it an immutable Latin and Christian culture. Second, its independence was inspired by the French Revolution's rationalism and liberalism. Third, after independence and the establishment of the republic, Brazil's political institutions were influenced by the United States.[101]

This blend led him to the following judgments on the general outline of Brazilian foreign policy: "To look outside of the Western world for a political model would be a violent break with our ethnic, religious, cultural, and sentimental origins. Therefore, no doubt remains: we are Western by reason of our political origin and by the . . . force of our spiritual aspirations." [102] Further, belonging to the West meant assuming the burdens of alliance: "Our obligation is already taken. Our attitude ought to be in favor of a courageous and enlightened struggle." [103]

But FEB officers never argued for an altruistic internationalism. General Golbery do Couto e Silva pointed out that the West needed Brazil, its resources, its human potential, and its geographic position in the South Atlantic. He shrewdly added that, although Brazil is dependent on Western assistance, that aid is in the direct interest of the West to give—a Communist Brazil would be a geopolitical disaster.[104]

In the mid-1950s Meira Mattos expanded this notion of reciprocal obligation. Writing at the time of the Tenth Inter-American Conference, Mattos advised the Brazilian delegates not to ignore the fact that the U.S. Latin American economic policy from World War II to the early years of the Eisenhower administration had been unjust. Specifically, he charged that during World War II a price ceiling was placed on Latin American exports to the United States while the price ceiling was

---

[101] Carlos de Meira Mattos, *Projeção Mundial do Brasil* (Rio de Janeiro: Biblioteca do Exército Editôra, 1959). Selections were reprinted in the *Boletim de Informações,* July 1961, pp. 14-18. The *Boletim* was put out by the army general staff and remained under the control of the FEB officers. Much of it was devoted to foreign policy.

[102] *Boletim de Informações,* pp. 14-15.

[103] Ibid.

[104] Golbery do Couto e Silva, "Problemas da América Latina: O Brasil e a Defesa do Ocidente," *A Defesa Nacional,* April 1959, p. 114.

removed for United States products to Latin America. He concluded by stating that, since Western Europe had recovered from the war, it was time for the Americans "to give concrete proof that Pan-Americanism is not a rhetorical expression." [105]

On the sensitive issue of foreign investment in Brazil—the *bête noire* of the romantic nationalists—the FEB group has been generally tolerant. For example, the military journal, *A Defesa Nacional,* stated its approval of foreign investment because it improved living standards and, therefore, improved national security.[106] The *Boletim de Informações,* published by the army general staff, encouraged the entry of foreign capital because it gave Brazil access to the latest technology— a matter of obvious importance to the military.[107]

Later, after the revolt of 1964, the moderate officers directly defended themselves from the charges of *entreguismo.* The *Boletim de Informações* argued editorially that the repeal of the Goulart profit remittance law would not make Brazil a vassal to foreign corporations. In fact, said the journal, a good investment climate would encourage reinvestment of profits. It also noted that in 1965 Brazil had the lowest remittance rate in Latin America.[108]

The FEB officers also saw opportunities beyond the Western world, and the area that fascinated them most was Africa. Like the civilian intellectuals, they ignored Latin America, but unlike them, they tended to be less euphoric (and less vague) about Africa's promise. They see Africa as a trade rival rather than as a trade partner. Meira Mattos has argued, for example, that Africa, as an economic rival, is "highly prejudicial to Brazil's foreign trade." [109] And he added: "The economic development of Africa will represent for us a sudden loss of European and North American markets for our classic export products, since Africa can produce similar substitutes with a much cheaper labor force. . . ." [110]

---

[105] Carlos de Meira Mattos, "Mosáico Internacional," *Revista do Clube Militar,* January-February 1954, pp. 49-50. In these years, the Clube Militar was controlled by the moderate-conservative officers.

[106] *A Defesa Nacional,* September 1955, p. 107.

[107] *Boletim de Informações,* August 1958, p. 5.

[108] "Capital Estrangeiro no Brasil," *Boletim de Informações,* November 1966, pp. 23-25.

[109] Carlos de Meira Mattos, "O Brasil e o Despertar Afro-Asiático," *A Defesa Nacional,* June 1960, p. 114.

[110] Ibid., p. 116. A more optimistic note was struck by Alcio Chagas Nogueira, who played down the problem of trade competition and stressed similarities be-

But Meira Mattos did not leave it at that. Rather, he argued for more contacts with Africa, so that at a later time it would not confront Brazil as an "uncomfortable and dangerous neighbor." [111] Closer to the point perhaps, Meira Mattos also suggested that the African market might be ideal for Brazilian industrial goods and that the trade rivalry would be eased if Brazil depended less on primary products exports.[112] Another FEB officer, Colonel Aryton Salguiero Freitas, essentially agreed with Meira Mattos's analysis, but added that Brazil could create sympathy and, perhaps, future markets in Africa through small amounts of technical assistance to African countries, especially in West Africa.[113]

But FEB intellectuals have more in mind than trade when dealing with Africa. Meira Mattos, for example, has envisioned a mediatory role for Brazil: "We can carry out an important task of the true Western mission—the task of attempting to dissipate the anti-Western reactions of Afro-Asia." [114] Brazil, he believes, is in an especially good position to do this because of its traditional anti-colonialism and its lack of racism—both very familiar arguments.

But unlike many of his civilian counterparts, Meira Mattos was prepared to face the problem of Portuguese colonialism. He suggested that the Portuguese foothold in Africa might be turned to Brazil's advantage, since it could provide a natural opening. Unfortunately he left the exact formula for doing that to Itamaraty. [115]

Two years later, *A Defesa Nacional* was less hopeful. It acknowledged that Portugal was in serious trouble in Africa. Much of the blame, it argued, could be attributed to Lisbon's insistence on controlling everything from the metropole. This had the unfortunate result of preventing any training in African self-government. The journal then suggested that Brazil act as a mediator and conciliator and in some fashion assist Portugal and her colonies to redefine their relationship.

---

tween Brazil and Africa which could add to mutual understanding. His argument, however, is considerably less rigorous than Meira Mattos's. Alcio Chagas Nogueira, "Possibilidades de Intercâmbio entre o Brasil e o Mundo Afro-Asiático," *A Defesa Nacional,* May 1961, pp. 173-175.

[111] Meira Mattos, "O Brasil," p. 118.

[112] Ibid., pp. 116-118.

[113] Colonel Aryton Salgueiro Freitas, "O Brasil e os Estados Africanos," *A Defesa Nacional,* June-July 1961, pp. 127-128. Colonel Salgueiro fought with the FEB First Fighter Group in Italy.

[114] Meira Mattos, "O Brasil," p. 118.

[115] Ibid.

The article concluded, however, that the Portuguese, after losing Goa, were not likely to follow a more liberal policy. Nevertheless, Brazil should make the effort.[116]

Whatever the problems with Africa and Portugal, FEB officers have taken the prospect of a Luso-Brazilian world community seriously. Meira Mattos believes it is perfectly feasible to bring together the scattered Portuguese-speaking areas: "Distance disappears as an obstacle to the approach of these territories situated on opposite shores of the Atlantic Ocean." [117] Furthermore, according to his reading of world history, the future seemed to indicate that nation-states would be replaced by communities linked by similar traditions, ideology, and interests.[118]

To those who argued that Brazil would make it alone as a world power, Meira Mattos replied that few Brazilians shared this opinion; in fact, it was an opinion held more often by foreigners.[119] In contrast, he proposed a union of Brazil and Portugal "in a transcendental politico-strategic enterprise" which would become one of the multinational, multi-racial units that Arnold Toynbee has envisioned as the future great powers.[120] In the meantime, Meira Mattos said, Portuguese colonialism would be transformed by Brazil into a three-cornered community. And on this he proposed to build Brazil's African diplomacy:

> Through the Luso-Brazilian Community we could approach the new African nations, offering them our experience as a young nation with a recent colonial past which is just leaving the underdeveloped phase, which has not been burdened with racial problems, and which is interested in trade and economic ties with its neighbors across the Atlantic.[121]

Portugal transformed through the idealism of Brazil strikes Americans as naive and perhaps now anachronistic but it has captured the imagination of FEB officers who can neither reject Portugal outright nor accept it as it is. Meanwhile, Brazil's rapidly growing economic

---

116 "Portugal na África," *A Defesa Nacional*, January-February 1962, pp. 63-65.
117 Meira Mattos, *Boletim de Informações,* July 1961, pp. 19-21.
118 Ibid., p. 20.
119 Ibid.
120 He cites specifically Adolph Berle, *Tides of Crisis,* and the Frenchman, Tibor Mende, *Entre la Peur et l'Espoir*. Ibid.
121 Ibid., p. 21.

power and population may force an impoverished Portugal to look for substantial aid in preserving whatever influence it can retain in Africa.[122]

Any group with similar strongly held opinions as the FEB officers would quite naturally attempt to influence policy. In April 1964, they achieved what was for some the ultimate goal: making one of their own Brazil's president. Nevertheless, their principal technique remained the same: instilling their beliefs and values in the officer corps.

Thus, while the left-wing nationalists placed great value in winning the Clube Militar elections and placing their own in senior field command positions, the FEB officers organized an all-embracing system of military education.

At its apex is the Escola Superior de Guerra (ESG), founded in 1949 by FEB artillery commander Cordeiro de Farias with the help of a U.S. advisory mission. The ESG provides an academic year's study on national security doctrine [123] and foreign affairs which was worked out by such FEB intellectuals as Golbery do Couto e Silva and Meira Mattos. The course included field trips throughout Brazil and ended with a twenty-day tour of the United States.[124]

Unlike its model, the United States National War College, the ESG includes both civilian faculty and students, with the latter representing more than half the school's graduates by 1970.[125] Mid-level officers

---

[122] Castelo Branco, as Brazil's president, endorsed an "Afro-Luso-Brazilian community," and felt it would be Brazil's economic power that would make it work. On the other hand, Brazil, he argued, could not merely endorse Portuguese colonial policy as it stood, nor could Brazil favor "premature Portuguese disengagement." From a speech given at Itamaraty to the graduating students at the Institute Rio-Branco and reprinted in *Textos e Declarações sobre Política Externa* (Rio de Janeiro: Ministério das Relações Exteriores, 31 July 1964), p. 12. The recent reverse in Portuguese policy in Africa has left the Brazilians with many problems and a few opportunities. At the moment, however, Brazil has only reaffirmed the Castelo Branco doctrine of favoring such a community on the basis of equality of all of its members. See *O Globo* (Rio de Janeiro), 9 May 1974, p. 15.

[123] See below, pp. 100-103.

[124] Schneider, *The Political System of Brazil,* p. 250; Stepan, *The Military in Politics,* pp. 177-178.

[125] The civilian student body was dominated by businessmen and civil servants (80 percent) plus an assortment of professionals, including economists, physicians, and Catholic clergy. The civilians play an important role in spreading ESG concepts by remaining in contact with new thinking through an active alumni association and by offering capsule versions of ESG doctrine in courses offered throughout the country. More than 200 of these were given in 1967-1969, and the number is increasing each year. Stepan, *The Military in Politics,* p. 178, and Schneider, *The Political System of Brazil,* pp. 250-251. See also Norman A. Bailey and Ronald M. Schneider, "Brazil's Foreign Policy: A Case Study in Upward Mobility," *Inter-American Economic Affairs,* Spring 1974, p. 9.

(colonels and brigadiers) of high academic standing are admitted to the ESG, and such an acceptance is now virtually a *sine qua non* for further advancement. Thus, while in 1955 only half of Brazil's senior generals were ESG graduates, the percentage climbed to 80 percent in 1962, and by 1970 the senior officer without ESG schooling was, in Ronald Schneider's phrase, as "rare as a one-legged soccer player." [126]

The FEB officers, especially since 1964, have not been content with just the ESG and its indoctrination of potential senior officers. By 1958 (with Castelo Branco in command) the army's general staff school for lieutenant-colonels was fully aligned with ESG doctrine and training methods. And in 1969, under the command of Meira Mattos, the army's military academy, Agulhas Negras, revised its curriculum to include far more in the social sciences, with the ESG's principal concept of national security through development serving as leitmotif.[127] In short, the FEB officers were not content with an occasional editorial in an army journal, but rather chose to combat romantic nationalism with a set of ideas systematically taught at nearly every level of the armed forces.

The resulting influence is unquestioned, but can the World War II-rooted experience of the FEB officers be passed on to the younger officer who has never seen first-hand the advantages of collaboration with the United States? The answer, of course, will not be clear for some years, but judging from the evolution of ESG doctrine, the emphasis on an American entente will be lessened though never completely abandoned.

In the meantime, it would be premature to write off the aging FEB officers as a direct influence in national affairs. It is true that Castelo Branco's presidential successors, Arturo Costa e Silva and Emilio Garrastazú Médici, were not members of the Expeditionary Force, but the current chief executive, Ernesto Geisel, was.[128] And even a number of key officers in the Costa e Silva and Garrastazú Médici administrations belonged to the FEB. Whether or not they continue to hold positions of power, their influence will continue to be felt for some time to come.[129]

---

[126] Schneider, *The Political System of Brazil,* p. 244.

[127] Ibid., pp. 250-251.

[128] See Robert M. Levine, "Brazil at the Crossroads," *Current History,* February 1973, pp. 53-56, for an updated account of the struggle for succession in Brazil.

[129] For a Brazilian appraisal of the FEB's success, see Umberto Peregrino, "O Pensamento da Escola Superior de Guerra," *Cadernos Brasileiros* (Rio de Janeiro),

The Linha Dura

The officers that make up the *linha dura* have evoked much comment but less is known about them than any other faction in the Brazilian armed forces. Yet their power is unquestionable, for they were able (among other things) to prevent Castelo Branco from choosing his own successor and to slow down his transfer of power from the military to civilians. But the precise extent of the *linha dura's* power and membership is still somewhat obscure.

The members of the *linha dura,* more than other politically active officers, have been known to switch factions or repudiate firmly held factional beliefs. Furthermore, there is no central career experience that unites them in the same fashion as the FEB group. The group seems to be a conglomerate of a few senior officers, several score colonels, and an unknown number of junior officers—apparently concentrated in the Rio-based First Army.

Perhaps the most convenient way of identifying the members of this faction is to spell out what they are not. They were not members of the FEB, they were not top graduates of their classes (and consequently few have had much to do with the Escola Superior de Guerra), few have served on the general staff, and few have academic or diplomatic links with the United States.[130]

The heart of the *linha dura* remains the colonels whose careers have stopped short of great success. Without combat service or high marks to propel them upwards in the military, and without the political favoritism of the João Goulart regime, these officers managed only very slowly to work their way up the ranks.[131]

November-December 1966, pp. 29-38. For a history of the ESG, see General Augusto Fragoso, "A Escola Superior de Guerra," *Segurança e Desenvolvimento,* no. 132 (no month given), 1969, pp. 7-40. *Segurança* is the official journal of the ESG.

[130] Alfred Stepan, in a small sample of five key officers in the Costa e Silva regime, found that four of them shared *linha dura* career variables described above. Stepan, *The Military in Politics,* pp. 249-250.

[131] Colonels Francisco Boaventura, Hélio Lemos, Almerindo Raposo, and Ruy de Castro have all been identified as key members of the *linha dura* by the Brazilian press. See *Jornal do Brasil,* 20 September 1967, p. 3; *Correio da Manhã* (Rio de Janeiro), 5 October 1967, p. 1. This last article stated that these same colonels were forming the "Green Lance Group," which would combat those who would betray the revolution. On the same day, the minister of war, Lyra Tavares (a FEB officer) prohibited under penalty of rigorous punishment any political com-

Older, more senior officers have also been identified with the *linha dura,* including, of course, Costa e Silva and Garrastazú Médici. Others include Odýlio Denys, Gabrielo Grum Moss, Silvio Heck, and Albuquerque Lima.[132] These senior officers are not really members of any well-integrated group, nor are they closely associated with the colonels. They belong to an older class of officers who hold on to their conservative, but highly nationalistic opinions, and act on them as individuals rather than as representatives of a faction within the military.[133] In general, the *linha dura* must be viewed as a group of older colonels who have more or less coalesced since the 1964 revolt, a group which is "still evolving and is still without organizational form." [134]

Unscrambling the *linha dura* ideology and foreign policy ideas is nearly as difficult as identifying and characterizing its members. The *linha dura* colonels, unlike the FEB officers, are not accustomed to working out ideas in systematic fashion. Indeed, their political strength in the past has been a passionate belief that Brazil's potential greatness was at stake, a view which has swayed many, especially the chronically impatient junior officers.

Bits and pieces can be inferred from their general view of things Brazilian. The hard-line colonels have consistently favored a sweeping renovation of Brazil's political and economic institutions to propel the

---

ment by any military officer. *Correio da Manhã,* 5 October 1967, p. 1. By 1970 a number of these colonels had been made eligible for brigadier general by sheer seniority. Schneider, *The Political System of Brazil,* p. 319.

[132] Generals Denys and Grum Moss, plus Admiral Heck, who were chiefs of staff under Quadros, refused to allow João Goulart to succeed to power. Albuquerque Lima, minister of the interior under Costa e Silva, was mentioned often as successor to Costa until his resignation from the cabinet in January 1969. His uncompromising authoritarian nationalism had endeared him to the hard-line colonels.

[133] See, for example, the actions of Generals Denys and Grum Moss and Admiral Heck in the presidential crisis of 1961. Skidmore, *Politics in Brazil,* pp. 206-216. The service chiefs were unable to line up support within the military to make their decision stick.

[134] Wilson Figueredo, "A Retirada do Linha Dura," *Jornal do Brasil* (Rio de Janeiro), 22-23 October 1967, p. 6. This Sunday supplement article is perhaps the best informed short piece on the *linha dura.* American observers have largely agreed with this journalistic assessment. Stepan has written: "This group was not entirely a fixed one, but one whose composition and passions changed according to the political pressures of the day." Stepan, *The Military in Politics,* p. 250. And Schneider has added: ". . . it may be helpful to consider the hard line as much as a state of spirit which could be accentuated by the course of events as a relatively small hard-core faction which under certain circumstances strikes a responsive chord in a broader spectrum of the military." Schneider, *The Political System of Brazil,* p. 218.

country into major power status by the turn of the century. They believe such a revolution must be carried out from the top by the military and that those in opposition should, at a minimum, have their political rights taken from them. This is necessary, they argue, because the politicians have proven both corrupt and inept in ruling Brazil. It is no wonder then the *linha dura* officers have bitterly opposed any plan for returning power to the civilians.[135]

Behind the *linha dura's* penchant for purging is a tense, volatile nationalism. The old politicians are despised because they sought personal gain at the expense of Brazil. The betrayal of Brazil's grandeur by the petty and the corrupt has proven unbearable to officers nurtured in the conviction that their country is a potential superpower.

This type of nationalism, of course, has its effects on foreign policy attitudes. In any situation in which the greatness of Brazil is called into question, the *linha dura* officers will vigorously lobby for nationalist measures. This may well involve actions directed at Western countries, including the United States. There is some evidence that during the 1967-1969 Brazilian-American conflict over U.S. importation of instant coffee, it was the *linha dura* that placed pressure on the Brazilian president and Itamaraty not to make any concessions during the negotiations.[136]

Officers identified with the *linha dura* have been outspoken on other "nationalist" issues. Colonel José Costa Cavalcanti, Costa e Silva's minister of mines and energy, has pushed for an independent atomic energy development program, and General Albuquerque Lima has lobbied for development and integration of the Amazon by capitalizing on the widespread Brazilian fear that the area might be lost to foreign powers unless Brazil acts decisively.[137] The former president, Garrastazú

---

[135] This was especially true after the state elections of 1965, when *linha dura* officers wanted to void a number of elections. They did not get all they demanded, but they were able to decide who would succeed Castelo Branco. The restiveness was also apparent when the so-called *frente ampla*, a broad coalition of civilian politicians, began to take form. Stepan, *The Military in Politics,* pp. 248-250; Schneider, *The Political System of Brazil,* p. 262. They were also outraged at the Brazilian Congress for permitting Deputy Moreira Alves to remain undisciplined after his alleged insult of the armed forces. Frances Foland, "The Prospects for Brazil," *The New Leader,* 20 January 1969, pp. 5-8. It may be assumed that the *linha dura* officers are no happier over the results of the recent (November 1974) congressional elections. But the results will probably be accepted, because, although the opposition party posted large gains, the Brazilian Congress remains politically impotent.

[136] Berilo Dantas, *Última Hora* (Rio de Janeiro), 13 November 1967, p. 2.

[137] Schneider, *The Political System of Brazil,* pp. 215-216.

91

Médici, has incorporated the Amazon development idea into his "Project Brazil: Great Power" scheme.[138]

To be sure, the *linha dura* periodically employs such catch phrases as "defending the Western Christian world against atheistic and Eastern Communism," but their only real anticommunism is directed at the domestic Communist threat.[139] Thus, the hard liners, unlike the FEB officers, do not look upon the Western community as a regularly interacting system of nation-states, but as a group of independent states vying with each other for commercial and political advantages. And it is for Brazil to assert its presence without timidity.

Linha dura techniques are not especially subtle. By and large, they have not tried very hard to inculcate their views in the classroom except at the Junior Officers' School in Rio de Janeiro.[140] Instead, they have attempted to force their opinions on policy makers, and occasionally they have succeeded in imposing their wishes, especially when they were able to mobilize otherwise legalist officers on emotional, nationalist issues. Thus, they have helped to prevent the return of civilians to complete control and have steadily whittled down civilian participation in government. In foreign policy, they have imposed their own highly nationalistic viewpoint on an ad hoc basis.

The Military's Influence

The Brazilian military was directly involved in politics long before 1964, and it is not likely that it will withdraw from it in the near future. Since World War II, morever, the armed forces have taken an even greater interest in foreign policy, due in part to the always blurred line between foreign policy and national security. But Brazil's military has gone beyond a broad definition of national security.

The military's views on foreign policy would be decisive if there were military unity. However, different factions have defied discipline and articulated their own separate policies—all of which is quite unthinkable at Itamaraty. In 1964, the left-wing nationalists were virtually

---

138 Ibid., p. 324.
139 Hélio Jaguaribe, "A Renúncia do Presidente Quadros e Crise Política Brasileira," *Revista Brasileira de Ciências Sociais* (Rio de Janeiro), November 1961, pp. 272-311.
140 That is, the Escola de Aperfeiçoamento de Oficiais. Stepan, *The Military in Politics,* p. 250.

eliminated through forced retirement of scores of officers. But the surviving factions flourish, and, given time and a civilian government, romantic nationalism may appear again. That kind of fervent nationalism is too deeply rooted in Brazil for it to disappear easily.

In the meantime, the *linha dura* will continue to lobby for a more nationalist line of its own, and the FEB group will seek to perpetuate its influence through a continuation of systematic indoctrination in its security-development-foreign policy doctrines at nearly every level of the armed forces.[141]

In closing this part of the discussion, it is worth noting that there has been a dilution of the FEB group's internationalist views with decidedly more nationalist notions. The change began in earnest in 1967 under ESG commandant, General Augusto Fragoso. According to one observer: "The *idée fixe* of the inevitability of a Third World War was substantially softened if not abandoned. In its place there began to emerge a concept of Brazil's shared interests with the other developing nations, particularly in the area of trade and atomic energy." [142]

Thus, it seems that both the *linha dura* and the left-wing nationalists, with little forethought but high passion, have made their mark. It seems likely that in the next decade, with the passing of the old generation of officers, a more united officer corps, trained in increasingly nationalist ESG doctrine, will emerge. In that case, the military's views should be decisive, despite Itamaraty's discipline and the respect accorded to it by the outsider. It may well be that the foreign ministry's chief influence on the broad lines of policy will be through its access to the Escola Superior de Guerra and the sharing of its special expertise with the military command.

---

[141] This influence has not been confined to the military and a select group of civilians. In April 1969, an ESG style course in Brazilian studies was offered at the Federal University in Rio de Janeiro. Beginning in 1971 the ESG's alumni association announced plans to increase substantially its efforts to spread the national security doctrine. Schneider, *The Political System of Brazil,* pp. 327 and 338.

[142] Ibid., pp. 256-257.

5

U.S.-Brazilian Relations:
The Emergence of the
Hemisphere's Second Superpower

In recent years Brazil's foreign policy has focused on developmental-nationalist themes; those policies with the highest priority are those that directly tie in with the country's drive for development and its quest for major power status. *Directly* is the operative word.

In contrast, the Quadros-Goulart years produced no such integrated, coherent strategy. Policy was either a matter of symbolic gestures (decorating Che Guevara) or the vague aspirations of that curious animal of contemporary international relations, the middle-range power.

As a self-conscious member of that by no means exclusive club, Brazil made disarmament one of its major diplomatic efforts in the early 1960s. The rationale was twofold: (1) preventing a nuclear exchange was in everyone's interest, and (2) reducing arms expenditures would free resources in the developed countries to be made available for the underdeveloped.

As a whole, however, the policy smacked of the unreal. No convincing argument was made to show that outsiders could be particularly effective in easing the Soviet-American standoff, and Brazilian diplomats simply did not have the expertise to assist in any actual negotiations between the superpowers. Brazil was left with pious and usually tautological exhortations ("nuclear war is a bad thing") at the United Nations. Further, the circuit between reductions in arms spending and increased foreign aid is so indirect and filled with so many points of resistance that such an enterprise as Brazil's disarmament effort was dubious at best.

Consequently, the more sober, tough-minded men of the later-1960s reduced the emphasis on such goodwill offerings and placed priority on policies that would directly benefit Brazil. Two issues are of particular interest because (1) they are likely to affect Brazilian-American relations in the future, and (2) because, while they seem unimportant to Americans, even faintly ridiculous to well-informed specialists, they are of extreme importance to a wide spectrum of politically active Brazilians. These issues are the development of the Amazon Basin and the building of an independent Brazilian nuclear capability.

Development of the Amazon

Brazilians have always taken great pride in the vast Amazon Basin, and they have also been highly suspicious of foreign interest in the region.[1] The first is understandable; the latter, although intimately tied with the former, requires more explanation.

The region drained by the Amazon River constitutes the immense heart of the South American continent. It includes no less than 60 percent of Brazil's great land mass, 67 percent of Colombia and Bolivia, 50 percent of Peru, a good slice of Venezuela, the southern extremities of the three Guianas, and a portion of tiny Ecuador.[2] The Brazilian Amazon alone covers nearly 2 million square miles, and with a population of only eleven million, the region has a population density of only 5.5 persons per square mile. There are vast stretches of the basin where the actual density is *one* person for every thirty square miles!

Economically, the Amazon region has been described by Herman Kahn as a Type C area, which means it is virtually untapped and, to a large extent, quite literally unexplored.[3] Living is on the subsistence level, and the small amounts of investment that do exist are small, extractive, and unintegrated.

The Amazon region is the world's largest unused land reserve. It is rich, untapped, and therefore highly vulnerable—according to Brazilians. In the words of a report prepared by the Escola Superior de

---

[1] See above, pp. 13-14.

[2] Herman Kahn and Robert Panero, "Novo Enfoque sobre a Amazônia," *Revista Brasileira de Política Internacional,* March-June 1968, pp. 59-60.

[3] Ibid., pp. 56-57. Area A is designated the industrialized urban core, like São Paulo, which Kahn argues has more in common with its counterparts in the U.S. and Western Europe than its own rural areas. Area B is a modernized seventeenth century society, an agricultural base "with a superstructure of tractors, crop-dusters, mechanics, public works and a little of modern mining." Ibid., p. 56.

Guerra: "The Amazon therefore borders seven nations while at the same time being underpopulated, without adequate transportation and communications, with a high rate of illiteracy, poor sanitary conditions, and rudimentary economy that cannot produce enough food for its own subsistence." [4]

For Brazilian strategists the development of the Amazon Basin has become a vital national security problem with pronounced foreign policy overtones. Precisely what and whom do the Brazilians fear, and how do they plan to resolve the problem?

In combing the literature, one finds two broad themes. First, the Amazon is an area of incalculable wealth which may very well guarantee the future greatness of Brazil.[5] Second, the region is vulnerable to no less than three different foreign threats under the general rubric of "international greed" (cobiça internacional), a phrase made popular by Arthur Cezar Ferreira Reis, a former governor of the state of Amazonas and now an influential academic.[6]

The most immediate, although much less serious, threat is the traditional one posed by Brazil's Amazon neighbors: Bolivia, Peru, Colombia, Venezuela, Guyana, Surinam, and French Guiana. The total length of the Amazon frontier is nearly seven thousand miles, much of it trackless wilderness, and there is a clear hint in this age of realpolitik that the treaties worked out by the Baron Rio-Branco are no longer sufficient guarantees of Brazil's borders. As early as 1943, a decree law declared it government policy to populate the frontier, and in 1959 a system of military-run settlements was created. One of the principal purposes of this system was to "create and fix nuclei of national population at places along the frontier where prosperous areas are located in a neighboring country as well as certain means of communication (navi-

---

[4] "Uma Política de Segurança Nacional para a Amazônia: Estudo Especial da Equipe da Escola Superior de Guerra," *Revista Brasileira de Política Internacional,* March-June 1968, p. 105.

[5] A report prepared by the Escola Superior de Guerra in 1968 states: "It is clear that the Amazon is on the world level, above all, a matter of demographic politics. It is the vastest and most peaceful of the open spaces still left on earth; it is ecologically useful in the production of animal and vegetable foodstuffs; its topography and morphology offer no obstacles; it possesses a bearable climate for men of any ethnic origin; it does not require the dislocation or conquest of native or aboriginal populations because it is an empty land." Ibid., pp. 110-111.

[6] His book *A Amazona e a Cobiça Internacional* went through two editions (Rio de Janeiro: Cia. Editôra Nacional, 1960, and Rio de Janeiro: Editôra Limitada, 1965).

gable rivers, roads or open country) that give free access to the national territory." [7]

The second type of threat seen by Brazilians is posed by the super-powers. According to Brazilian historiography, in the nineteenth century both British and Americans were eager to open the Amazon for world trade and for their own commercial interests.[8] In the twentieth century, the problem, if anything, became more serious. The developed countries are in constant search for new raw materials and new areas to develop, and, worse, they possess the military power to support their needs.

It is little wonder then that rumors have spread and charges have been made about North Americans in the Amazon. One current in 1967 held that the Pentagon had prepared a contingency plan for transporting millions of American survivors of a nuclear holocaust to the Amazon in order to re-create the Anglo-Saxon republic. Several years later, another widely accepted rumor had it that U.S. officials were planning to use the area as a dumping ground for Negro militants.[9]

Serving as a catalyst for these speculations was the study on Amazon development prepared by the Hudson Institute and first presented to the Brazilian government in 1965. Although the scheme has undergone changes through the years, the institute's plan still calls for the damming of the entire Amazon River with a low (fifteen to twenty-five meters) earthen dam, at a cost of $800 million. This would result in the creation of an inland sea one-third the size of France.[10] The Amazon dam, according to its proponents, would create the planet's largest and cheapest source of hydroelectric energy.[11] It would, accord-

---

[7] "Uma Política de Segurança Nacional," p. 108.

[8] Arthur Cezar Ferreira Reis, "Por Que a Amazônia Deve Ser Brasileira," *Revista Brasileira de Política Internacional,* March-June 1968, p. 9.

[9] Robert B. Panero, "A Dam Across the Amazon," *Science Journal,* September 1969, p. 56.

[10] Ibid., pp. 56-57. Robert Panero and Herman Kahn, "New Focus on the Amazon," Hudson Institute Paper HI-758-P, 1 July 1965. The latter essay appeared in the *Revista Brasileira de Política Internacional,* March-June 1968, pp. 51-64. Dr. Panero has also suggested that similar, but smaller, dams be built on the Amazon's tributaries in order to create a "great lake" system that would draw all of South America closer together through water transport. Robert Panero, "On the Use of Low Dams as a Possible Stimulant to South American Development," Hudson Institute Paper HI-788-RR, 10 January 1967.

[11] Why install such a capacity in an area where there is virtually no demand for power? Panero seems to argue for a gradual increase in capacity and the construction of giant transmission lines to Rio de Janeiro and even Buenos Aires. The cost of such a project is not estimated, although there is a hint that the technology for such an enterprise is not yet developed. Panero, "A Dam Across the Amazon," pp. 58-59.

ing to the plan, revolutionize communications in the interior, as massive water transportation (including twenty-thousand-ton ships) would be made possible throughout much of the continent. It would provide easy access to now untouched minerals (for example, bauxite deposits along the Surinam-Guyanese-Brazilian border) and equally inaccessible timber resources. A fishing industry could be developed, and, for the first time, flood-controlled agricultural lands would be opened up.[12] The scheme is obviously empire-building on a majestic scale, although its author does cite some problems: negative ecological side-effects and difficulties in financing the project.[13]

Brazilians have been generally unenthusiastic about this proposal.[14] In a "secret report" prepared by three Brazilian diplomats for Itamaraty, the Hudson Institute as well as its scheme received heavy criticism.[15] It is on two levels. First, there was the prima facie suspicion of any scheme advanced by the institute, whose principal occupation is advising the American government on its security problems.[16] The diplomats' report admits that no clear link has been established between the Amazon plan and American security, but they are certain that the suspicion is legitimate, and they advance indirect evidence in support of it: The moving force behind the project, Robert Panero, has family ties in Colombia (he is married to a Colombian). The director of the Inter-American Committee for the Alliance for Progress (and a Colombian diplomat), Carlos Sans de Santamaria, requested the Hudson Institute to prepare plans for Latin American development. And two of the great lakes which would be created in Colombia under Panero's plan would provide a navigable passage between the Atlantic and

---

[12] Ibid.

[13] Ibid., pp. 59-60.

[14] Hudson Institute's director, Herman Kahn, has upset Brazilians on other grounds. He has, for example, expressed doubt as to Brazil's ability to achieve superpower status in the foreseeable future. Indeed, Kahn projects that Brazil will not achieve a per capita income of $3,600 until the year 2097. (He contends that India, starting from a smaller base, will do so in 2084; and Brazil's rival, Argentina, by 2036.) Herman Kahn and Anthony J. Weiner, *The Year 2000* (New York: Macmillan, 1967), p. 149.

[15] The report was leaked to a Rio daily, *Correio da Manhã*, 14 July 1968.

[16] The institute was also roundly denounced by four Brazilian congressmen in the Chamber of Deputies on 12 February 1968, led by the leader of the opposition party. Reprinted in *Revista Brasileira de Política Internacional* under the title "O Grande Lago Amazônico e o Hudson Institute," March-June 1968, pp. 148-165.

77616

Pacific oceans—that is, an alternative to the Panama Canal would be created.[17]

The Itamaraty report also examined the scheme itself, finding what were interpreted as numerous flaws: The flooding would wipe out agricultural land of recognized value and destroy existing industries, principally jute and rubber. It would inundate cities "which represent national bulwarks against the new and growing efforts of foreign interests in the area." [18] Ecologically, the climate would change, the flow of sediments into the Atlantic Ocean would be stopped, and perhaps the earth's center of gravity would alter under the additional weight of dammed up water on the equator.[19]

But underlying all these criticisms is the fundamental objection to the scheme: It entails the internationalization of the Amazon. Even if Brazil participated vigorously in such a multinational development effort, it would be giving up ultimate control over its own national territory.

It is apparent from the diplomats' report that the institute's assumption that Brazil would be interested in *continental* integration and regional development is very much mistaken. Brazil wants to maintain its own identity, and doing so means fostering national development plans, an effort the report explicitly recommends for the Amazon in order to counter the appeal of the Hudson Institute's "Grand Vision." [20]

In addition to fear of Brazil's neighbors and the U.S., some have raised the spectre of the underpopulated Amazon being forcefully occupied by surplus population from poor, overcrowded countries. A report from the Escola Superior de Guerra specifically warns against complacency on this issue and proposes that "a national policy of planned and methodical occupation of the Region be adopted with the objective of marking it—the whole area—with the characteristics of our civilization and effectively integrating it in the national framework." [21] One can, then, easily imagine the consternation among some Brazilians when Kenneth Boulding suggested the following in a work translated into Portuguese:

17 "A Verdade sobre o Instituto Hudson," *Revista Brasileira de Política Internacional,* March-June 1968, pp. 138-139.

18 Ibid., p. 147.

19 Ibid., pp. 139-140.

20 Ibid., pp. 140-141.

21 "Uma Política de Segurança Nacional," p. 110.

If, for example, we suppose that 200 million Asians established in the Amazon Valley, in the next 25 years, the resources freed in Asia could be sufficient to raise the levels of life and nutrition drastically enough, in order to produce the desired cut in fertility. However, migration on this scale is inconceivable in *the present world situation*, and if Asian countries and others like them attain a society of a high technical order, they must do it by methods very different from those used to produce that kind of society in Europe and in the United States.[22]

Brazilians are, for the most part, strongly opposed to any multinational development scheme for the Amazon. They are as protective toward this treasure house as the imperial officials were in the nineteenth century. At the same time, Brazilians fear the region cannot be retained until it is completely integrated into the economic and political life of the nation.[23]

The Amazon and National Security

The major problem is economic development. The Amazon Basin is far from achieving self-sustaining growth. Indeed, it is far behind even Brazil's impoverished Northeast. The region, in short, is not a focus of growth. Private as well as public investment continue to receive a much higher return in already developed areas of the country.

But as Dias Mendes puts it, the issue involves more than the short-run efficient allocation of scarce resources. The primary objective is "to maintain Brazilian sovereignty over the area," and economic rationality cannot take precedence. Moreover, the Amazon itself can provide a fresh mystique for countryside development. According to Dias Mendes:

> The construction of Brasilia with its projection in the exterior, played up to a point this role. . . . People are used to following "flags"—appeals that move them to action, and that through

---

[22] Quoted in Armando Dias Mendes, "Amazônia: Desafio e Contribuição," *Revista Brasileira de Política Internacional,* March-June 1968, from Kenneth E. Boulding, *Princípios de Política Econômica* (São Paulo: Editôra Mestre Jou, 1967). Despite Dias Mendes's alarm at Boulding's hypothetical solution to Asian overpopulation, he does compare Brazil's nondevelopment of the region to the "anti-social, unproductive great landowner." Ibid., p. 28.

[23] This is the assumption of both Ferreira Reis, "Por Que a Amazônia," p. 12, and Dias Mendes, "Amazônia," p. 28.

these same slogans their reserves of enthusiasm are truly directed. What other objective is there when men speak of a "new frontier," "the great society," "the national grandeur"? [24]

The Brazilian government has apparently taken up this suggestion. The Escola Superior de Guerra continues to make hand-picked members of the economic and political elite aware of the region. In addition, the Costa e Silva and the Garrastazú Médici administrations have made efforts to make younger Brazilians Amazon-conscious. To overcome the region's aura of remoteness, in 1967 the government initiated Project Rondon. According to one Brazilianist:

> Carried on twice a year, in January-February and again in July, this rapidly growing program now involves more than 10,000 students a year and has been extended to nearly all of Brazil's frontier areas as well as the interior of major rural states. Its purpose is to acquaint students with the Brazilian reality "and to gain their support for a program of less talk and more action"; in short, it is a challenge to students to work for the country's modernization and development rather than to denounce the present system and call for its violent demise. Along these lines measures under consideration during the second half of 1970 would make all Brazilians of draft age subject to service in some activity linked to national development and security, with many of them to be employed in massive literacy campaigns.[25]

But the regime has not been satisfied merely with publicity-propaganda. Since 1970, Project Brazil, the country's ambitious master plan for development, has included as one of its three major projects the construction of the Trans-Amazon highway which is designed to open up the jungle for permanent settlement.[26] The highway stretches 5,000 kilometers and runs from Recife, capital of Pernambuco, and João Pessoa, capital of Paraiba, along the southern bank of the river to the western frontier.[27] It is expected that along the road would come

24 Mendes, "Amazônia," p. 27.

25 Schneider, *The Political System of Brazil*, pp. 326-327. A more detailed, but basically skeptical, account of Project Rondon can be found in Jon Rosenbaum, "El Proyecto Rondon: Un Experimento Brasileño de Desarrollo Económico y Político," *FORO Internacional*, October-December 1969, pp. 136-148.

26 The other two projects are development of the Northeast and export promotion. *The Japan Economic Journal*, 18 September 1973, p. 15.

27 This would seem to end any chance for an Amazon Sea. Plans for another Amazon highway further north, running from Amapá state (which borders French Guiana) to the Colombian border, are now being studied. Ibid.

hundreds of thousands, perhaps millions, of immigrants from the densely populated, impoverished Northeast. Thus, not only would the problem of the latter region be solved (at least in part), but the empty spaces of the Amazon would be filled with Brazilians. To finance all of this, the Amazon Development Bank has been created and will probably receive steadily larger grants of capital from the central government.

In the meantime, Brazilian strategists, despite the difficulties they will face in executing these vast projects, will no doubt continue to be suspicious of foreign interest—even foreign assistance—in developing the region. Although foreign investment may continue to be welcome in developed areas like São Paulo, the welcome will always be much less warm in the Amazon.

Brazilians recognize the difficulties in conquering the Amazon, although on the whole they remain optimistic, and probably over-optimistic. Nevertheless, as Albert Hirschman has recognized, it is useful, perhaps essential, that they minimize the real difficulty and move ahead anyway.[28] The alternative is honest but fruitless discouragement and the preservation of the status quo—and that Brazilian leaders, and in time perhaps the Brazilian people, will find intolerable.

The New Nuclear Policy

Brazil's determination to be something more than a middling power is very apparent in its atomic policy. Briefly, Brazil has refused to sign the 1967 Nuclear Non-Proliferation Treaty (NPT) and has insisted on maintaining its freedom to develop a nuclear capability, albeit for peaceful, developmental purposes.

Our present purpose is to examine the new Brazilian nuclear policy, draw out the often unstated implications of that policy, and determine, if possible, how much is rhetoric and symbolic gesture and how much is substance?

To understand Brazil's atomic program, it is helpful to consider how Brazilian strategists now view the world. Fortunately, that view was fully expressed by a senior diplomat (and former foreign minister), João de Araujo Castro, in a recent lecture delivered at the Brazilian

---

[28] Albert O. Hirschman, *Development Projects Observed* (Washington, D. C.: The Brookings Institution, 1967), pp. 7-34.

embassy in Washington.[29] According to Araujo Castro, the United States and the Soviet Union are attempting to freeze the present configuration of world power, that is, the bipolar world as it emerged in the wake of World War II. It is not clear whether he considers this a conscious policy of the two superpowers, but the ambassador does state explicitly that since the Cuban missile crisis there has been a tacit understanding between the U.S. and U.S.S.R. to avoid "the exacerbation of crises and tensions in determined areas that are considered of special interest to one or the other." [30] That understanding, he notes, has survived Vietnam, Czechoslovakia, and even the Middle East. The détente has survived because the two powers share a common interest: the freezing of the worldwide distribution of power. At this point, Araujo Castro is careful to state that power includes not only military, but economic, political, and scientific-technological aspects as well. The superpowers, in short, want to "institutionalize the inequality between nations." [31] Strong nations wish to remain powerful because they assume they have a monopoly on responsibility, prudence, and moderation, and, conversely, the weak powers are immature, erratic, and irresponsible. Allowing the latter to accumulate power, therefore, would be dangerous to world peace.[32]

To maintain their monopoly, the superpowers are more and more fostering policies on a wide range of matters that go beyond the "survival agreements" of the 1960s. In economics, Araujo Castro charges, both have followed policy lines that would prevent the underdeveloped nations from ever catching up. Both (but especially the Soviets) have opposed effective multilateral aid programs, and with the waning of the cold war, they have also reduced their bilateral assistance.[33] Further-

---

[29] Araujo Castro's statement is all the more remarkable, since this articulate, former foreign minister and ex-ambassador to the United Nations argued eloquently for general and complete disarmament in the early 1960s. See his *Desarmamento, Desenvolvimento, Descolonização* (Rio de Janeiro: Ministério das Relações Exteriores, 1963).

[30] Araujo Castro, "O Congelamento do Poder Mundial," *Revista Brasileira de Estudos Políticos,* January 1972, p. 11.

[31] Ibid., p. 13.

[32] Ibid., pp. 12-13.

[33] Araujo Castro's wrath is especially directed at the socialist countries which, he charges, have embraced the principles of economic liberalism. He adds: "It is said that in preparing to attend any meeting of the Social and Economic Council on the Second Committee of the U.N.'s General Assembly, the socialist delegates take the elementary precaution of leaving in the vestibule all their books by Karl Marx." Ibid., p. 16.

more, both have resisted tenaciously any effort to revise their trade policies toward the poor. In the meantime, they have attempted to divert attention away from the issue by raising the alarm over alleged dangers to the environment from industrialization. He notes that the World Bank under Robert McNamara has even threatened to refuse loans on projects that do not take into account their ecological side-effects.[34]

Araujo Castro contends that the lance point of this superpower condominium is the Nuclear Non-Proliferation Treaty negotiated bilaterally by the Soviet Union and the United States and presented peremptorily to the rest of the world. The ambassador further suggests that the two superpowers buffaloed the non-nuclear nations into signing the treaty without giving them adequate time to think through their national self-interest regarding nuclear development. In the meantime, after "disarming the already disarmed," the super nuclear countries continue to make no progress whatever on general and complete disarmament—Brazil's long-held goal. In fact, he charges, the very object of the SALT talks has never been nuclear disarmament at all, only "the elimination of over-over-kill." Thus, the U.S. and U.S.S.R. achieved their shared aims: preserving the core of their military power, establishing procedures to prevent a holocaust, and preventing others from getting nuclear weapons.[35]

With this world view, what should Brazil do? Most obviously, that country must resist any attempt to keep the world bipolar. It should specifically press for revisions in trade policy, maintain its claim to a 200-mile sea limit, and resist any attempt to impose ecological standards on its own development.[36] Within the U.N., it should continue to lobby for amendments to the charter. "We cannot live eternally in the year 1945," remarks Araujo Castro. "All attempts to immobilize and congeal history are futile and laughable." [37]

---

[34] Ibid., pp. 18-19.

[35] Ibid., pp. 13-15.

[36] "Underdevelopment," Araujo Castro remarks, is "one of the worst forms of environmental pollution." Ibid., p. 19.

[37] Ibid., p. 15. Nevertheless, Araujo Castro also stresses continued good relations with the U.S. In a recent speech he said: "The essential thing is that we conduct our relationship with the United States without worrying about whether to agree with them in the name of loyalty and some old tradition, or to disagree just to show independence or maturity. Brazil no longer needs to proclaim its independence every day of the year and every hour of the day." Quoted in *Visão* (São Paulo), 4 November 1974, p. 28.

This then is the strategic context in which Brazil's nuclear policy was formed during the last half dozen years: Brazil will resist being contained as a strategically vulnerable nation. The world's distribution of power must not and cannot be frozen.

Despite Araujo Castro's confident analysis, Brazil's strategic planners took several years to work out the new policy. President Castelo Branco, for example, expressed some doubts about the Latin American nuclear-free zone treaty because it compromises hemispheric defense of Panama and Puerto Rico, and not because it harms Brazil's interests directly. Later, however, his more nationalistic foreign minister, Juracy Magalhães, hinted that non-proliferation would not be accepted by the non-nuclear powers because of a superpower diktat. But by 1966 Brazilian officials were announcing their first concrete objection to the non-proliferation treaty. At a U.N. disarmament conference in that year, Ambassador Antônio Corrêa do Lago announced:

> Among the reservations which could be made to the treaty, there is the fear that the non-nuclear Powers, by signing it, would not only be giving up the possibility of having the most dreadful weapons man's imagination has ever devised, but, at the same time, would be foregoing the benefits which derive from the peaceful uses of atomic energy.[38]

Still, Brazil did not adopt a policy of complete nuclear independence until Artur da Costa e Silva's inauguration as Brazil's second revolutionary president and the appointment of conservative, but highly nationalist, José de Magalhães Pinto as foreign minister. At the new president's first cabinet meeting, he emphasized that an important priority of his administration was "Brazil's intense participation in the scientific and technological revolution of our day." Nuclear energy, specifically, he argued, would be one of the most powerful tools in that revolution and in the production of its primary product: economic development.[39]

Three weeks later, Costa e Silva spelled out more precisely Brazil's nuclear policy. At the new Palácio Itamaraty in Brasilia, he repudiated the acquisition of atomic weapons, claiming to be fully aware of the dangers of their dissemination. But, he added, those risks cannot be

---

38 Quoted in Jon Rosenbaum and Glenn M. Cooper, "Brazil and the Nuclear Non-Proliferation Treaty," *International Affairs* (London), January 1970, p. 77.

39 From the minutes of the first cabinet meeting, Brasilia, March 1967, and reprinted in the *Revista Brasileira de Política Internacional,* March-June 1967, p. 7.

used as an excuse to prevent the peaceful use of atomic energy. If his government did that, Brazil "would be accepting a new form of dependence, surely incompatible with out aspirations for development." [40]

In June 1967, speaking at a new hydroelectric plant site, Costa e Silva declared:

> The Brazilian Government will reserve the exclusive right as far as the installation and operation of nuclear reactors as well as research, mining, manufacturing and sale of nuclear minerals and mines . . . and special fissionable materials. It will create conditions in this country and abroad for the development of technical and scientific personnel specializing in the field of nuclear energy on the advanced and middle levels in the quantity and on the terms necessary for scientific research which will be intensified within the national territory.[41]

Why have the Brazilians changed policy? There are two major themes to their rationale. First, there is the fear of being permanently left behind in the technological race. Costa e Silva's foreign minister argued, for example, that *the* most important gap developing between the rich and poor nations is not per capita income or military strength, but one involving the accumulation of scientific and technological knowledge. If Brazil is to complete the industrial revolution it began in the nineteenth century, if it wants to avoid being "a mere importer of techniques" and "an eternal payer of royalties," then it must resist all attempts "to institutionalize . . . in international treaties our present economic and technological inferiority." [42] And since the most rapid innovations are taking place in the fields of space and nuclear energy, it follows that Brazil must also concentrate on those areas or remain forever dependent on technological handouts of the mighty.

---

[40] Costa e Silva, speech, 6 April 1967, in ibid., p. 8.

[41] Costa e Silva, speech, 30 June 1967, in ibid., p. 9.

[42] José de Magalhães Pinto, speech to Brazilian scientists, 7 June 1967, in ibid., pp. 9-10. Also, Ambassador Sérgio Corrêa da Costa, then secretary-general of Itamaraty and possibly the most technologically informed Brazilian diplomat, once stated: "The Brazilian Government is firmly convinced that technological underdevelopment is without a shadow of doubt the most complicated and onerous form of dependency with which we find ourselves. The full national emancipation now is not obtained by simple force of arms as happened in the nineteenth century or by an increase in GNP as occurred even in this century. A country will only be independent . . . if it does not resign itself to scientific neo-colonialism and it demonstrates a capacity to develop its own technological solutions." Sérgio Corrêa da Costa, speech to the Faculty of Law, University of São Paulo, 29 May 1967, in ibid., p. 47.

In addition, Brazilians have expressed a collateral fear: the nuclear powers will attempt to keep Brazil from catching up by imposing conditions on their technical assistance. Thus, while they are willing to permit experimentation with nuclear reactors or radioisotopes, the superpowers are unwilling to assist on large-scale projects involving nuclear explosives. "It is as if they asked us to stop making dynamite because it can be used for war purposes," argued one senior Brazilian diplomat. Or, he added, it is as if "they tried to stop us from making vaccines because the same technology that the Oswaldo Cruz Institute uses could be employed for bacteriological warfare." [43]

The solution to scientific inferiority and what is perceived as superpower foot dragging is an all-out Brazilian effort in the nuclear field.[44] But the fact remains an autarkic nuclear development policy would be incredibly expensive.[45] How do Brazilian officials calculate the payoffs? According to them, they are nearly limitless. For example, in a country where fuel oils are still imported in large quantities, nuclear power plants will supply the electrical power to serve a rapidly expanding industrial base. The search for atomic minerals will help open up the remote areas of the country. Radioisotopes will be used in agriculture and to improve the quality of manufactured goods—a technique

---

[43] Sérgio Corrêa da Costa, interview with *Última Hora*, 28 June 1967, in ibid., p. 57.

[44] The Brazilian rationale as presented here comes entirely from the open literature. Two American observers, Jon Rosenbaum and Glenn Cooper, have pieced together from their interviews with Brazilian officials other reasons for the new atomic policy. Basically, it is argued that the NPT entrusts the strategic defense of Brazil permanently to the U.S. No self-respecting power, it is alleged, can ever accept this. Although the same officials have pledged publicly not to develop nuclear weapons, the previous argument is obviously inconsistent with this position. But since Brazilian nuclear policy is shrouded in secrecy anyway, outsiders may well be skeptical about any Brazilian public statement. In any case, either policy reflects the major thesis of this essay: namely, the Brazilians perceive themselves as a potential superpower, and anything or anyone that impedes that objective will be opposed with any argument at hand. Rosenbaum and Cooper, "Brazil and the Nuclear Non-Proliferation Treaty," pp. 80-81.

[45] One estimate is that, with an all-out effort, a respectable stockpile of bombs would accumulate by 1980. The cost would be hundreds of millions of dollars. Ibid., p. 78. The estimate does not include the price of a delivery system. But it should be remembered too that Brazil (with the help of NASA) has a large rocket research program. According to the judgment of a group of Brazilianists: "The general conference opinion was that Brazil could conceivably acquire a crude nuclear delivery system in this decade and that such a development would cause considerable concern among her neighbors." "Brazil's International Role in the Seventies: A Conference Report," *Orbis*, Summer 1972, p. 553.

vital in maintaining trade competitiveness.[46] Later, when Brazil makes its own fissionable material, it will have the ability to manufacture its own nuclear explosives. At that point, the payoff begins in earnest. Giant engineering works are foreseen: rivers will be made navigable, canals dug, ports deepened, minerals uncovered, and petroleum extracted.[47]

Two specific proposals are worth mentioning. One would employ atomic explosives to connect the Amazon with the Plata and Orinoco rivers, thus effectively integrating the interior of Latin America.[48] The second would transform the miserable Brazilian northeast. According to Frances Foland:

> With giant nuclear reactors as cores, agro-industrial complexes at four sites—Recife, Natal, Fortaleza and São Luis—would produce electric power for evaporators to desalt water in sufficient quantity to turn arid lands into farm lands. The power would also feed factories and smelters for processing fertilizers, chemicals and ores. The four complexes could accommodate some 20 million people, over two-thirds of the region's total population. Whereas each of these complexes might cost $1 billion and involve gigantic transformations in the physical and human configurations. Brazil has already undertaken the feasible with the scheduling of a 1969 construction of its first nuclear-power center to produce 500,000 kilowatts.[49]

Despite these glorious visions of the future, Brazilians have also been sensitive to current criticism of their nuclear policy. The most common complaint by foreigners has been that there is no real difference between nuclear devices for peaceful use and nuclear weapons. The world only has Brazil's pacific assurances, it is alleged; there is no other guarantee.

In response, it is argued that the point made has substance, but it is essentially of a polemical nature, and that is not enough to stop Brazil's nuclear program. It is further argued that, while nuclear explosives are both sword and plowshare, their production in useful

---

[46] Corrêa da Costa interview in *Última Hora*, pp. 60-61. See also an interview with Admiral Otacílio Cunha, former chairman of the National Commission on Nuclear Energy, in *Última Hora,* 19 May 1967, in *Revista Brasileira de Política Internacional,* March-June 1967, p. 73.

[47] Sérgio Corrêa da Costa, *Manchete,* 15 April 1967, in ibid., pp. 51-52.

[48] Ibid., p. 55.

[49] Foland, "Whither Brazil?" p. 55. Brazil's first nuclear-power reactor will begin operating in 1977.

numbers is a different process. The manufacture and accumulation of weapons require great secrecy, while peaceful bombs could be open to inspection by any number of outside inspectors. Indeed, Ambassador Corrêa da Costa has gone on record proposing "adequate systems of control that won't restrict our scientific development nor expose us to industrial espionage." [50]

Behind this riposte, however, is an ill-concealed impatience with the superpowers. In effect, it is argued, the established nuclear nations are telling Brazil it cannot be trusted with the atom. It is unstable and less responsible—a banana republic somehow grown too large. [51]

Brazil's Nuclear Capability. The Brazilians are rapidly acquiring an impressive nuclear capability, despite a slow start. Brazil will have its first nuclear plant by 1977, while Argentina's first plant began operations in 1973. [52] A second Brazilian plant is planned for only four years later. At the moment, Brazil is not capable of producing atomic explosives, although it has been estimated that it will have such a capability by 1980. What is acutely lacking now is engineering skill and the capacity for making fissionable material. [53]

Brazil is quickly acquiring the necessary industrial base, it has vast open areas for testing, and it apparently possesses enough proven reserves of thorium and uranium to be one of the few countries self-sufficient in atomic minerals—and exploration has only just begun. [54]

[50] Corrêa da Costa, speech to the Faculty of Law, in *Revista Brasileira de Política Internacional,* March-June 1967, p. 49. Long-time arms control buffs could, of course, quickly sketch out many loopholes in the ambassador's statement negating any chance for adequate inspection.

[51] See Corrêa da Costa's interview in *Manchete,* in ibid., p. 52. See also John R. Redick, *Military Potential of Latin American Nuclear Energy Programs* (Beverly Hills, Calif.: Sage Publications, 1972), pp. 18-19.

[52] Another problem has been Brazil's difficulty in retaining its nuclear scientists. In recent years, however, the government has launched a campaign which subtly combines patriotism and material incentives. There is as yet no evaluation of its success. Rosenbaum and Cooper, "Brazil and the Nuclear Non-Proliferation Treaty," p. 78.

[53] Foland, "Whither Brazil?" p. 44. Uranium has been found in Minas Gerais and Guanabara. More recent discoveries were made in the Northeast, especially in the Maranhão-Piauí Basin. Rosenbaum and Cooper, "Brazil and the Nuclear Non-Proliferation Treaty," footnote, p. 78. Meanwhile, funds for exploration increased five times in 1970, and they have been going up at a rate of some 40 percent since them. *Uranium: Resources, Production and Demand* (Paris: Joint Report by the OECD Nuclear Energy Agency and the International Atomic Energy Agency, 1973), p. 32.

[54] Rosenbaum and Cooper, "Brazil and the Nuclear Non-Proliferation Treaty," footnote, p. 84.

Research facilities currently are small, but of first-rate quality. The three principal institutes are in São Paulo (Institute of Atomic Energy), Rio de Janeiro (Institute of Nuclear Engineering), and Belo Horizonte (Institute of Radioactive Research).[55] All three are equipped with reactors, and the newest in Rio (completed in 1965) was the "first totally constructed in Brazil by Brazilian engineers, technicians and workers."[56]

In addition to its own resources, Brazil has uranium purchase agreements with Portugal. It has also signed technical assistance treaties with the U.S., Canada, Germany, France, and Israel. Brazilians seem particularly hopeful about the Israeli and French accords. Both countries have agreed to joint research projects, and the French are specifically interested in exploration for uranium, manufacture of nuclear materials, and training of Brazilian scientists and technicians.[57] Thus, even if the U.S. were to cut back on its assistance program, others would find it in their self-interest to support the Brazilian program.[58]

Public Opinion and Nuclear Development. In the meantime, the Brazilian government has found that the independent nuclear policy is a popular one. In a government-sponsored poll, 89 percent supported the government's policy, while only 3 percent believed Brazil "must subject herself to the demands of the atomic powers."[59] Thirty percent felt Brazil should use nuclear energy for all purposes, including weapons, a high percentage in view of the fact that this is not official policy as yet.[60]

The nominal opposition party, the Movimento Democrático Brasileiro, has supported the government's policy and so have a number of powerful newspapers which usually oppose the regime. Domestic criticism has been confined to a few newspapers like the *Estado de São Paulo* and the *Jornal do Brasil* plus some members of the Castelo Branco administration—chiefly the ex-minister of planning, Roberto Campos,

---

[55] General Uriel da Costa Ribeiro, chairman of Brazil's atomic energy commission, in an interview with *Última Hora,* 17 May 1967, reprinted in *Revista Brasileira de Política Internacional,* pp. 62-64.

[56] Corrêa da Costa in ibid., p. 49.

[57] Rosenbaum and Cooper quote unnamed Brazilian officials who claim to be unimpressed with American nuclear assistance and not overly concerned about losing it. Rosenbaum and Cooper, "Brazil and the Nuclear Non-Proliferation Treaty," p. 82.

[58] Quoted in ibid., p. 83.

[59] Ibid., footnote, p. 83.

[60] Ibid., p. 84.

and the former ambassador to the U.N. (and now editor of the *Jornal do Brasil*), José Sêtte Camara.[61]

Brazil has the resources and probably the long-range commitment to develop nuclear explosives by the early 1980s. The United States has little influence that it can exert over Brazil on this question, and, since the late 1960s, has refused to exert what influence it has.

Meanwhile, the Brazilian nuclear policy, though questionable on a cost-benefit basis, has been an increasingly prominent part of Brazil's new foreign policy. The policy successfully combines national pride with economic promise, and Brazil will not be deterred by appeals to the common good of humanity. Thus, while others view the Nuclear Non-Proliferation Treaty as one step in the direction of arms control, if not disarmament, Brazilians see it as largely irrelevant to peace and as a device to limit the number of superpowers in the world.

---

[61] Ibid., footnote, p. 81.

6

America's Brazilian Policy for the Future

The United States, possibly within a decade, probably will be faced with the problem of dealing with Brazil as an emergent power in the hemisphere. Brazil has a strong national identity and a talented elite. By 1985 it should have a highly developed industrial base and a rapidly modernizing agriculture, which will be supported by an increasingly sophisticated technology adapted to Brazilian circumstances. How Brazil will play the role of a major actor on the world stage must, of course, be of concern to the United States. Brazil could continue its traditional friendship with us or it could strike out in another direction. At best, a "Gaullist" Brazil could provide us more than a few uncomfortable moments.

Any future policy toward Brazil must confront these additional issues: First, how do we live with an authoritarian regime that, at least in its early years, the United States was willing to support at nearly any cost? Second, do we select Brazil for special treatment and risk further alienation of the Spanish-American republics?

American Policy of the Recent Past

Before answering these interrelated questions, it might be wise to sketch out Washington's current Brazilian policy, what other options are being discussed, and what is right, wrong, and plain inadequate about all of them. Present U.S. policy is still very much in the doldrums, following a period of very active and successful policy making, largely fashioned in the field by two extraordinary American ambassadors, Lincoln Gordon and John Tuthill. After the coup of April 1964, the United

States committed itself to a massive rescue operation reminiscent of the Marshall Plan (in which Lincoln Gordon had a major role). The total aid program shot up, and, indeed, in the mid-1960s it was the third largest American foreign aid program after Vietnam and India. Clearly, Brazil had become a priority concern.

Lincoln Gordon's successor, John Tuthill, finished the task by recognizing the dangers of an extended and heavy commitment that was beginning to irritate Brazilians and bother Americans. An enormously visible American presence and close identity with the regime was an increasing embarrassment to both sides, and John Tuthill's "Operation Topsy" seemed the way out. Its object was simple: cut heavily into American personnel, especially in the AID program. Reductions of up to 40 percent were made between 1967 and 1969.[1]

Following Gordon and Tuthill in the ambassadorial position came a string of thoroughly competent, professional diplomats, but they were unable "to spell out a comprehensive program of U.S. government priorities in Brazil," as John Tuthill himself had suggested.[2] They all seemed rather relieved that the emergency was over, pleased with the success of American and Brazilian efforts, and quite uncertain what to do next. In testimony to a Senate subcommittee, former ambassador to Brazil, William Roundtree, asserted: "The importance of Brazil in hemispheric affairs, and indeed, in world affairs is indicated by its size, its population, its economy, and the rapidity with which it is progressing as a real economic power in the region."[3] But the ambassador would not go beyond that. Unfortunately, American statesmen had been saying for decades similar things, but recognition of importance, potential or actual, is not a policy unless one is content with merely watching it grow.

If the men in the field in recent years seem a little lost, what about officials at the top? On the basis of the public record alone, the last five years have been very lean. Only two references to the importance of Brazil by high officials can be found. The first, from President Nixon, was directed at his visiting Brazilian counterpart, Emilio Garrastazú Médici. In perhaps an unguarded moment, the American President said

---

[1] The details of this operation can be found in Ambassador Tuthill's own account published in *Foreign Policy,* Fall 1972, pp. 62-85.

[2] Ibid., p. 85.

[3] U.S. Congress, Senate, Subcommittee on Western Hemisphere Affairs of the Committee on Foreign Relations, *United States Policies and Programs in Brazil,* 92d Congress, 1st session (May 1969), p. 290.

"as Brazil goes, so will go the rest of the Latin American continent." [4]
Critics, here and abroad, have teased out enough wretched implications
from these words that it is unnecessary to add any others. But it seems
closer to the mark to say that one can make nearly anything one wants
to out of this cryptic compliment, and more importantly, it says almost
nothing clear about American policy toward Brazil.

Far more revealing (if all too brief) was then Secretary of State
William Rogers at a news conference held in Brasilia following talks
with the Brazilian president. The secretary, after describing an exchange
of views on world problems and bilateral matters, concluded: "We
don't have any problems really, at the moment, at all between Brazil
and the United States." [5] Nothing could indicate better the present
outline of high policy: Brazil is doing fine. There are no difficulties
now. Future ones (if any) may be settled on an ad hoc basis—the kind
of thing mature partners do. In short, Brazilian-American relations after
a period of storm and stress have settled down to a comfortable, slightly
dull domesticity.

The one last high official whose views are worth considering is
Jack B. Kubisch, former assistant secretary of state for Latin American
affairs. Some had hoped that this assistant secretary, with his field
experience in Brazil (as deputy AID director), would take the lead in
outlining a firmer policy. But in public, at least, he did not suggest any
departures from the Rogers dictum.

Aside from the public record, there are reports of the President's
personal correspondence with President Médici. And Henry Kissinger
is reported to be on close terms with Foreign Minister Azeredo da Silveira
and his predecessor, Mario Gibson Barboza. Moreover, within the State
Department there is a recognition that Brazil's extraordinary growth
means a different relationship emerging in the next five to ten years.
Brazil's importance, now and in the future, is clearly understood, but
what should be done about the country is never really spelled out.

In Search of a New Policy

But if policy toward Brazil has not produced a host of specifics, it is
dealt with by implication through administration statements on Latin

---

[4] Quoted from the *Department of State Bulletin,* 3 January 1972, p. 13.
[5] Quoted from the *Department of State Bulletin,* 25 June 1973, p. 915.

America. The reigning formulas begin with statements warmly extolling the uniqueness of each of the region's two dozen republics and pointing out the dangers of lumping them together for the sake of generalization. Once that is understood, a special American relationship for the entire area is asserted, based on history, geography, "and other forces" which have shaped a wholly unique community of nations.

The United States side of the relationship involves no hegemonial ambitions. Furthermore, we seek only friendship (but only to those who want it); we support development efforts and regional integration, but we shall avoid imposing our standards of performance on anyone. We offer in the meantime no slogans and no promises we cannot keep.[6] And in doing this we shall establish "a mature partnership" with Latin America. Of course, it could be easily argued that "no slogans" is another slogan, and, worse, promise keeping is easy when no promises are ever made. But such a complaint would surely be off target. More to the point is the following: the establishment of a mature relationship with nations that range from the miniscule to the small in the world balance of power is an unlikely enterprise at best, and all the more unlikely in view of the frequent complaint by our European allies that we have not treated *them* as mature partners.

Worse still, and more immediate to our purposes, these oft-repeated guidelines are apparently intended for Haiti as well as Brazil because we still see the area as a coherent whole, with Brazil very much part of the region. Thus, despite the administration's rhetoric about heterogeneity, it clearly does not inform our actual (or perhaps more accurately our announced) policy.

But despite these preliminary criticisms, it would be a mistake to simply believe that current Brazilian, much less Latin American policy, is maximally bad, and should therefore be flogged without mercy. Actually, and especially in light of such unilaterally conceived and executed fiascos as the Alliance for Progress, this is not such an awful set of operating assumptions. But the problem remains: what is probably good for Bolivia might not be particularly good or relevant for its big next-door neighbor, Brazil. The facts are that Brazil is not small, undeveloped, of limited potential, or politically unstable. Furthermore,

---

[6] See, for example, Assistant Secretary Jack B. Kubisch's speech before the Council of the Americas in Washington on 6 June 1973 and reprinted in the *Department of State Bulletin,* 9 July 1973, pp. 68-71.

116

its Portuguese culture removes it—indeed, at times, has isolated it—from its Spanish-American neighbors.[7]

Two more preliminary remarks are in order. First, I do not want to launch into that familiar specialist's plea about paying attention to our "neighbors." Indeed, the premise of that school of thought is that we owe them something, a priori, although the moral basis of that claim is not clear. It is not at all clear, for example, to the U.S. Congress, which remains the political institution that best expresses the interests of the American people. In fact, the "moral claim" of our Latin American neighbors can only be easily accepted if it is assumed that the unguided and personally painless altruism of the few is superior to the expressed wishes of Americans—a strange doctrine indeed.

Besides the moral ambiguity, there is the probably insurmountable problem of administering large aid programs effectively over a long period of time.[8] But that is another subject. In Brazil's case any critique of present policy must be on the basis of self-interest: we, in short, owe it to ourselves to re-think our relations with Brazil.

The Opportunity. It is in our self-interest for two reasons. First, the United States and its real partners, Japan and Western Europe, have an opportunity to help integrate Brazil into the developed, neo-capitalist, Atlantic community. Secondly, that community could keep Brazil from turning into a kind of twenty-first century rogue elephant in its mad stampede for superpower status.

The second preliminary observation is this. Admittedly, a good argument for doing nothing now can be made. Surely, there is little that is more foolish (and dangerous) than an activist policy grounded in passionate ignorance. And in the absence of immediate problems, doing nothing will not seriously harm us or the Brazilians—at least for the immediate future.

The type of relationship that I argue for below will become possible only in the next decade. It would, I hope, be an approach that would

---

[7] Those who think of the difference between Spanish and Portuguese as trifling should review the relationship between the metropoles, Spain and Portugal. Their enmity is historic. In the New World it took an ironic twist. Here, it is the Spanish-American republics who have found reason to distrust the Portuguese-speaking colossus. On the Iberian peninsula, of course, it was little Portugal which had to fend off Spanish ambitions.

[8] For a rare independent audit of American aid programs in Mexico and Central America, see the account of William C. and Elizabeth Paddock, *We Don't Know How* (Ames, Iowa: Iowa State Press, 1972).

have the same sense of purpose that our Brazilian policy had in the recent past. And in offering this strategy, I would stress opportunity rather than threat in the coming decade. It is not an unlimited opportunity to be sure, but it is that middle-level, nonevangelical sort of thing that no one need go through a fundamental upheaval to achieve, but which would be of some, even great, benefit to the Western world.

Brazil as a Problem. But before outlining this future opportunity, we should examine the difficulty America experiences now in relating to the Brazilian regime: can we even talk about future opportunity with a government that so many find repugnant?

It remains a delicate problem despite the American (albeit reluctant) accommodation to the regime. For one thing, reaction in Europe (which is critical for Brazil's future) has not been so benign. In the press, and even among officials, open hostility is expressed toward the Brazilian government for its military-style authoritarianism and, more specifically, for its use of torture on captured "revolutionaries."

A number of initial (and partial) responses can be made to this. First, the reaction to Brazilian political behavior is, to put it mildly, selective. We need go no further than non-Communist Europe itself. Greece and Turkey are not models of political virtue, and never have been. And even more specifically, Gaullist France's war of extermination against the Organisation Armée Secrète was no less determined (and extralegal) than Brazil's war on urban terrorists.

There is the possibility that the problem will resolve itself in the next decade. For one thing, the regime may become less obviously military in nature. The selection by the top military leadership (and thus election) of a civilian president may happen in 1978, for example. More importantly, the use of torture may be eliminated entirely when all levels of government in Brazil become convinced that the terrorist bands represent no serious threat to the regime. One certainly can be suspicious of the bland historicist assumption that all polities can do nothing but progress (at least over the long haul). But Brazil is truly an ambiguous case. It could go either way, and what Americans and Europeans do will probably have great, perhaps even decisive, impact.

The Basic Decision. But these observations do not meet the issue squarely. To do that we must make choices, assume risks, and understand more clearly what we are about.

First, we must decide whether or not the regime will last or be blown out of power like the Greek colonels. The present regime may change in some respects, of course, but it is my assumption that radical change is unlikely. In the first place, there are few if any alternatives to the present regime. The self-styled revolutionaries have no chance. They represent no one and are politically inept. The previous generation of civilian politicians is very unlikely to regain power. Its members are either too old or have little popular support today. Indeed, the only likely "alternative" to the present is a turn to a more purely military, more authoritarian regime. Such a shift could be in response to future economic difficulties or, less likely, internal as well as external pressures to return power entirely to the civilians.

Not only are the alternatives improbable, but the regime's chances for survival have grown, not decreased, in the last decade. This has happened despite the preferences of foreign, especially European, governments. Since 1964 Brazil has undergone four successions, each less traumatic than the previous, and since a peaceful, orderly transfer of power is always difficult to manage in any polity, Brazil's increasing success at it suggests more about the regime's durability than a gaggle of other less important socioeconomic and political variables that one could chase around.

A few of the latter, though, are worth mentioning in passing. The last two administrations have won middle-class support by promoting rapid economic growth and by achieving a reputation for being comparatively free from corruption. Furthermore, both have identified themselves with the most buoyant aspects of Brazilian nationalism—something which obviously has widespread appeal.

If the United States must accept the regime as permanent (as I think it has done) then we need to examine the proposition that the U.S. should transform it into something more acceptable in our sight. The assumption, hardly ever questioned, is that a military government is unacceptable to us and most Brazilians, although the latter have not as yet seen fit to do much about it.

Unfortunately, the moral imperative to do something is vague, but it can be dealt with on general principles. It would be wise, for example, to ask ourselves if doing something is likely to improve Brazil's chances for political decency. More bluntly, can we force the regime to accept our standards? The experience with sanctions is also not very encouraging. Supposedly vulnerable Rhodesia has not yet submitted to international pressure, nor have the other *bêtes noires* of contemporary world politics, Portugal and South Africa. And within our own hemisphere, the military junta of the extremely vulnerable Dominican Republic was not persuaded, despite heavy American pressure, to restore "democracy" after the removal of Juan Bosch from the presidency in September 1963.

Pressure on Brazil? In addition to the question of success, there is the knottier problem of utility. The reaction within Brazil to such pressure must be weighed. As we have seen, Brazil does have a volatile nationalism, and any overt, hostile act on our part could well undermine those Brazilians who want to re-establish elective, civilian rule in the country. And, unfortunately, many of the most touchy nationalists are precisely those who do not care if civilians ever regain power.

The most publicized aspect of Brazilian politics involving the United States is, of course, the oft-repeated allegation that torture has "in fact become an intrinsic part of the governing process." [9] And no other issue is more singularly complex. How widespread is it? How many truly innocent are involved? Who in fact is doing it? Has it declined since the apparent high tide of protest in 1969-1970? What role has the U.S. played? I doubt there are definitive answers to any of these questions. Nevertheless, a few observations should be made.

First, a skilled apologist for the Brazilian government might argue that precious few regimes in this world have an abiding respect for the individual's legal rights. And further, if we are truly concerned over acts of physical torture, why are we so appallingly selective in our protests. Why have we not bombarded the Soviet Union with indignation? Why do we have to wait for an Alexandr Solzhenitsyn to prick our consciences?

This approach has its merits, but it does overlook at least two important considerations: Brazil is a friend and ally as clearly as the Soviet Union is not, and one should always be more concerned with the moral behavior of one's friends than of one's enemies. Also, for the Soviets, the use of torture is no aberration. This is not true for Brazil, and this suggests it would be more amenable to U.S. concern.

What is the extent of torture in Brazil? I do not know. That it exists is certain. One of the problems is that the information about it is

---

[9] Stepan, *The Military in Politics*, p. 262.

not reliable. For example, a principal source for torture stories is the so-called Brazilian Information Front, headquartered in Algeria and staffed by political exiles, many of Marxist inclination. But by March 1971 even this highly partisan source had only assembled a total of 120 cases of police and military torture.[10]

Protests from the Roman Catholic church, including Pope Paul VI, are to be taken more seriously, although, again, they tell us little of the scope of the problem. Parenthetically, it is a bit puzzling that highly secular critics of the regime are so quickly willing to ascribe infallibility to any clerical pronouncement on the matter. Apparently in this particular case the Pope cannot be bamboozled. But that aside, the clergy, especially within Brazil, are more satisfactory witnesses than the political exiles.

The heart of the matter for us, however, is the extent of U.S. involvement. The argument that general American support for the regime means somehow shared responsibility for every act of that regime can be rejected out of hand. Only if the United States were omnipotent could it even think about assuming the burden of righting every wrong in the world.

A more credible criticism, however, is our support for the so-called (now terminated) "public safety" program, which, among other things, trained over 600 members of the newly organized Federal Police between 1959 and 1972. The United States has, of course, flatly denied any advocacy or support of torture. It has instead repeated its concern directly to the Brazilian government.[11]

Is there any other evidence besides American denials? The torture accounts indicate that most of it seems to be carried out by the intelligence and security branches of the armed forces (especially the navy) and state police (especially São Paulo's Força Pública and its Department of Political and Social Order). The former have never been included in the U.S. training program and state police forces were largely phased out of it by 1968.[12]

---

[10] *Washington Post,* 7 March 1971, reprinted in U.S. Congress, Senate, Subcommittee on Western Hemisphere Affairs, *United States Policies and Programs in Brazil,* pp. 305-307.

[11] See, for example, the statements of State Department spokesman, Carl Bartch, in press briefings on 21 April and 23 July 1970. Ibid., pp. 292-293. For details of the public safety program, see ibid., pp. 3-5, 21, 33, 50, 241, 279, and 282.

[12] Ibid., p. 4.

But whatever the amount of American involvement, the issue itself cannot be dismissed with a shrug of helplessness. On the other hand, bold, public, and official warnings from us are not likely to produce positive changes within Brazil. The United States is left with quiet diplomacy and a hope that the regime is committing itself to the elimination of mistreatment of prisoners, even those who are themselves practitioners of murder, kidnapping, and robbery for political ends.

The U.S. and Revolutionary Regimes. Underlying much of the uneasiness at close American-Brazilian relations is the feeling that the United States has failed to live up to its revolutionary traditions by supporting conservative-reactionary military dictatorships and, of course, by being hostile toward "revolutionary" regimes. The issue, although often badly argued, does get to the heart of what we are about as a people: is our system grounded in revolution? That is, are we revolutionary? The answer turns on what we mean by revolutionary.

In the American case, revolution asserted political independence based on the "self-evident" truth that all men are created equal, and therefore possessed of certain inalienable rights. But in declaring a condition of natural equality in these rights the Founders were not attempting to abolish natural inequalities or certain conventional inequalities (for example, property). Indeed, the Constitution was designed to secure the enjoyment of such inequalities, and the American system of government rests on the assumption that certain conventional inequalities cannot be morally abolished by either government or by the mob. The United States is, in Joseph Cropsey's words, free "from the taint of misdirected egalitarianism" because "the democratic teaching of the Declaration and the Constitution contains nothing that is intended to afflict the conscience of wealth or power lawfully obtained and employed." [13]

Contemporary revolutions, by and large, are not founded on the American principle, but are tainted with "misdirected egalitarianism." Furthermore, as both the Cuban and Chilean revolutions demonstrate, they are based on antagonistic principles, which sanction unlimited police power and unlimited length of rule for a self-chosen few in order

---

[13] Professor Cropsey examines and criticizes four common arguments in behalf of foreign economic aid, and my analysis owes much to his insights. See Joseph Cropsey, "The Right of Foreign Aid," in Robert A. Goldwin, ed., *Why Foreign Aid?* (Chicago, Ill.: Rand McNally and Co., 1963), p. 123.

to eliminate conventional inequalities.[14] At no point do these revolutions and ours ever intersect.

It is obvious then that the U.S. cannot support such egalitarian revolutions or join in attempts to destroy regimes not based on such a principle without seriously compromising our own principles. The latter point needs amplification. If we must not confuse our revolution with others, can we impose our principles on regimes that are not in agreement with ours? Can we take measures against, for instance, a military dictatorship which finds life, liberty, and property as eminently alienable—especially when that dictatorship proposes to be our friend and ally? Should we, in short, attempt to make the Brazilians more like us?

Such an effort would constitute a kind of imperialism that would be either impractical (short of outright conquest) or dangerous (conquest means almost certain resistance, and, therefore, war). As Cropsey observes: "The conclusion is that we must be content to cultivate our own democratic vineyard and to sit in the shade of our constitutional doctrines without imagining that, because the Thirteenth Amendment follows from a truth about all men, it is *ipso facto* the guide to our action upon all men." [15]

Democratic imperialism itself is a contradiction in terms. A regime's legitimacy, which derives from the consent of the governed, cannot lightly impose a new form of government on a people who have not given their consent and who are not the responsibility of the imposing government in the first place. Such actions would seriously compromise a democratic regime's principles.

Most of the American Founders were quite aware of the danger of spreading our principles around the world by force of arms. Most, for

---

[14] Purists would argue that the Allende government was not self-chosen, that in fact it achieved power lawfully through the Chilean electoral process. That is true only to a point. Allende's coalition was elected by a plurality, not an absolute majority. More importantly, Allende did not propose to rule within the regime's basic framework for six years, but was intent on changing it fundamentally; he was, as he correctly claimed, a revolutionary. And nearly two-thirds of the Chilean electorate voted against his kind of revolution. In the meantime, the first "democratically elected" Marxist leader was using a wide assortment of quasi-legal (at best) police powers to cripple and eventually destroy his opposition. Only self-perpetuation in power could have been his objective, which is, to say the least, contrary to democratic practice. It was this intent, in fact, that brought the military out of the barracks in September 1973. See Robert Moss, *Chile's Marxist Experiment* (London: Newton Abbot, David and Charles, 1973).

[15] Cropsey, "The Right of Foreign Aid," p. 125.

example, were against aid to the South American revolutionaries in their war against Spain. Only a few, such as Hamilton (and he only briefly), were willing to risk American lives (and perhaps all-out war with a European power) for Latin American independence.

Not only were most of our first leaders convinced that war was dangerous, they also agreed that Latin America's chances of successfully adopting our principles were nil. Thomas Jefferson, for example, seriously doubted that republicanism was possible in societies marked by "the shackles of priesthood, and the fascinating glare of rank and wealth." [16]

Since then our resources have grown, but they are not infinite, nor are they sufficient to remake regimes. Even the smallest and most vulnerable (for example, the Dominican Republic) have remained stubbornly and successfully resistant to our sporadic attempts to make them "better." Only in the case of outright conquest and occupation (Japan and Germany) have we succeeded in significantly reshaping the political institutions of other nations.

Our duty then is not a universal one. We are not obliged to impose our principles on others. It is not practical and it is possibly self-defeating. On the other hand, we do have a duty to oppose (or at least not support) revolutions based on universalist principles that are hostile to ours.

This has been generally recognized throughout our history, and, therefore, the American system is and always has been a conservative one. It has fought to protect its own fundamental principles for the benefit of its own people and to provide living proof that there is a viable alternative to tyranny. This does not mean we should support someone else's status quo for the sake of their status quo. It does mean we should protect our own and leave others to their own vineyards.

---

[16] Koch and Peden, *The Life,* p. 681. John Adams was even blunter in his assessment. He rumbled to a friend that the "people of South America are the most ignorant, the most bigoted, the most superstitious of all the Roman Catholics in Christendom. They believe salvation to be confined to themselves and the Spaniards in Europe. . . . No Catholics on earth were so abjectly devoted to their priests, as blindly superstitious as themselves, and these priests had the powers and apparatus of the Inquisition to seize every suspected person and suppress every rising motion." With a people like that, argued Adams, the chance for free government was as absurd as "to establish democracies among the birds, beasts and fishes." Quoted from *The Works of John Adams,* ed. Charles Francis Adams, (Boston: Little, Brown and Co., 1856), vol. 10, pp. 144-145.

In the case of Brazil we should encourage it to follow the American example. But we are not its caretakers nor its enemies. Brazil is not threatening us, and it should not be treated as if it were.

Finally, it should be pointed out that not only would we harm ourselves directly if we acted contrary to our principles by pretending we were not a conservative power, but we also would not be believed and thus earn the well-deserved derision of the rest of the world. It might be added here that stout defense of principle will probably cost us dearly in the Third World and its champions among the developed countries. That is inevitable. The Jacobin illusion is widespread. It conveniently bestows legitimacy on self-chosen elites who either use it cynically to accumulate wealth and power (true of more regimes than most observers would care to admit) or sincerely in their efforts to build Utopia. We should remember that defense of principle has never been easy—we were a lonely outpost in the eighteenth century, and we may well be again in the twentieth. But the issue has not changed, nor the stakes.

A New Policy

But if we should not get into the business of fundamentally reshaping Brazil, what should be the basis of an American policy, a policy that is something more than a pleasant, bilateral amicability? First, it would be quite useless to return to old formulas, especially ones involving the provision of cheap, public capital. The external debt of Brazil alone probably makes this no longer a prudent policy, and American congressional disenchantment with at least bilateral aid programs is not ephemeral either.

The second trap to avoid is continuing to think of Brazil as a Latin American country. If we stopped doing that it would have two immediate benefits: First, it would foreclose any possibility that the U.S. would encourage Brazil to exercise any kind of "leadership" of the Spanish-American republics. The futility of this has been discussed above. Second, it would open the door for Brazilian membership in the Atlantic community. As such, it could join with the United States, Europe, and Japan—perhaps within the Organization of Economic Cooperation and Development (OECD)—to work out the economic problems and perhaps later the political problems all four will share in

125

the coming decade. Each is rapidly becoming interdependent, especially in trade; that is, their continued economic prosperity depends largely on selling to and investing more in each other.[17]

It is perhaps true at the moment that Brazilian membership in the OECD would rightly be questioned. There is a reported feeling within that body that since the admission of Australia and New Zealand the OECD has been stretched too thin. But Brazil's continued rapid growth would make admission virtually inevitable. It has already been invited into the Group of Twenty (along with Mexico and Argentina), and after another ten years the U.S. may well want to sponsor its inclusion in the Group of Ten.

But in any case, the American goal should be to widen membership in the community to include those countries which are neo-capitalist and making at least some effort to develop free political institutions. The necessary ties are already being made. Japan, for example, has quite deliberately selected Brazil as a prime source for raw materials and is following through with a heavy investment program.

Besides adding another dynamic economy to the community, Brazil's incorporation might help dissipate the notion of a Washington-Brasilia axis which is now accepted as true in many Spanish-American capitals. Brazilian integration would not be a matter of America dispensing unusual favors to Brazil; it would be a recognition by a number of nations that Brazil's international status has changed.

There are two assumptions attached to this argument. First, that present community difficulties do not destroy the community, leading to depression and a catastrophic decline in world trade. Second, and putting it in the negative, I am not assuming that Brazil's inclusion will lessen the sum total of the community's problems. Brazil will become a

---

[17] Anthony Eden has recently called for a new political community of major free nations on every continent, which would not duplicate NATO or, presumably, the OECD. It would include the U.S., Canada, the four leading West European nations, Japan, Australia and Brazil. He recommended that at the outset the members' foreign ministers meet three or four times a year to thrash out common political problems of a worldwide nature. Despite the problem of overcrowded schedules, he argued "that time and place must be found for such an organization if the free world is to survive and not fragment into disparate pieces without utility or authority." Eden's proposal stresses political problems, whereas the author's focus is on economic issues. If the latter are dealt with effectively, then the former has a chance of succeeding, and the political council will be more than a dialogue of the deaf. See Anthony Eden, "Getting the Free World Together," *New York Times*, 5 May 1972, p. 41.

participant in the ritualized hair pulling that is now and always will be at the heart of the community.[18]

And what of Spanish America? There is small possibility and less reason for another American grand unilateral handout to these countries. On the other hand, they should not be simply written off. There may be enough of a foundation for rapid economic growth if a real Spanish-American community were constructed. If sufficient incentives were offered, the Spanish-American countries might also be eventually integrated into the Atlantic community. But as separate republics with small internal markets, it is unlikely they will achieve healthy sustained growth, and that means their political and social problems will worsen, having a further negative effect on the economy. The American government, meanwhile, has an obligation not to ignore them entirely and not to flatter them with premature proposals for a mature partnership.

To return to Brazil, the emphasis of this proposal so far has been on the choices the U.S. and its partners must make in the coming decade. But Brazil faces some critical choices too. It may wish to act like a splendid, autarkic power or join with other nations of similar outlook. More immediately, it must finally choose between being a developed nation or continuing to act as a spokesman for the under-developed. At the moment, it can and does operate in two worlds, but even now its interests are more and more with the rich and not the poor of this world. It may rationalize its entrance into the Atlantic community by choosing to view itself as a special spokesman for the less developed countries, as the Italians have done within the European Economic Community in regard to Latin America.

There are encouraging signs that the present leaders of Brazil see their country primarily as a Western nation. But subsequent administrations may decide that the dubious value of Third World leadership is worth more than a junior partnership in the Euro-American club.

Integrating Brazil into that club is an idea whose time has not quite come. But until that moment, the United States has an opportunity to begin laying the groundwork for a new approach to Brazilian, and perhaps even Latin American, relations.

---

[18] Lincoln Gordon has also suggested that Brazil be "adopted" by the developed Western world, arguing that if Greece and Turkey could be members of the OECD so could Brazil. He adds: "True, the Mediterranean nations are there as a historical legacy from the Marshall Plan, but Spanish membership, and now Australian, have no Marshall Plan antecedents. The OECD is simply one symbol of many possible institutional adjustments." Lincoln Gordon, "Brazil's Future World Role," *Orbis*, Fall 1972, p. 631.